51 LESSONS FROM THE SKY

US AIR FORCE

FLETCHER MCKENZIE

51 LESSONS FROM THE SKY

NEAR MISSES AND STORIES FROM
51 PILOTS AND CREW FROM THE
UNITED STATES AIR FORCE

Copyright © 2018 by Fletcher McKenzie

A catalogue record for this book is available from the National Library of New Zealand.

All rights reserved. No part of this book may be reproduced in any form or by any electronic or mechanical means, including information storage and retrieval systems, without written permission from the publisher, except for the use of brief quotations in a book review.

First Edition

ISBN 978-0-9951170-13 (Paperback edition)
ISBN 978-0-9951170-06 (Ebook edition)

Published by Squabbling Sparrows Press
PO Box 26 126, Epsom, Auckland 1344
New Zealand

ALSO BY FLETCHER MCKENZIE

51 Lessons From The Sky (US Air Force)
61 Lessons From The Sky (Military Helicopters)
71 Lessons From The Sky (Civilian Helicopters)
81 Lessons From The Sky (General Aviation)
101 Lessons From The Sky (Commercial Aviation)

To Colonel Charlie Cook,

It was an honour to meet and interview you at the 2007 Reno Air Race. Spending time with you and hearing your stories from the many bombing missions during WWII was insightful. Hearing what you went on to achieve after your service was inspiring.

I raise a drink to you, to your crew and to Lady Luck.

Blue skies.

"It's your duty to fly the airplane. If you get killed in it, you don't know anything about it anyway. Duty is paramount. It's that simple if you're a military guy. You don't say 'I'm not going to do that - that's dangerous.' If it's your duty to do it, that's the way it is."

Brigadier General Chuck Yeager, USAF

CONTENTS

Foreword	xv
Introduction	xix
Prologue	1
HOW TO USE THIS BOOK	11
US AIR FORCE AVIATION SAFETY	13
1. PREPARATION & PLANNING	15
Wake Turbulence	17
There I Was…	25
Keep The Brief Sacred	29
Aircraft Strike Hazard	33
Electrostatic Discharge	39
2. COMMUNICATION	42
Deceptive Communications	43
Call Me On It!	47
Communication In C.R.M.	51
Ego Versus The E-Word	55
3. FATIGUE	60
Flying While Fatigued	61
Breaking The Error Chain	67
4. UNEXPECTED EVENTS	70
The Raccoon And The Rocket	71
5. IN-FLIGHT EMERGENCY	74
Murphy's Gunship	75
Say Something… Anything	81
Flight Emergency	85
Single-Seat Crew Duties	89
The Best $5 I've Ever Lost	93
Roll Your R's To ATC	97
Insidious Decompression	101
Full Throttle Or Go Home	105
Shaping The Ejection Decision	109

Compound Emergencies	113
Safe Landings	117
No IFE's	121
Emergency Comms	125
No. 2 Engine Bleed Air Leak	129
Imminent Engine Failure	131
No O2 At 41,000 Feet	133
Missile Warning	135
Catastrophic Engine Failure	137
6. COMPLACENCY	139
Haste Makes Waste	141
No Clearance Landing	145
Our Greatest Threat?	149
Flight Deck Habits	153
7. HUMAN FACTORS	157
Cross Country	159
Spatial Disorientation	163
Got The "ITIS"?	169
Air Refuelling Hazard	173
Fishing Boat In The Sky	177
Risk Vs Threat	181
Pushing Just To Check A Box	185
Close Call After Sunset	189
Go Green Or Go Home	195
A Lesson Re-Learned	199
8. WEATHER & ICING	205
Cold Weather Flying	207
Iced Up	211
Cold, Wet And Heavy	215
Thunderstorms	221
Common Sense	227
Cougar 21	231
9. FLIGHT ENVELOPE	235
The Ya-Ha Manoeuvre	237
10. FURTHER READING	240

Glossary	241
Acknowledgments	271
About the Author	279

FOREWORD
DAVID SHELLER

I never thought I would be a pilot, but life has a funny way of changing your plans. When I was young, I loved aviation but never thought of it as a possible career. However, I was lucky enough to be accepted into the United States Air Force Academy, and even further lucky to be graduating when there was a pilot shortage. At this time, if you didn't want to go to pilot training you had to go stand in front of a General and explain why you went to the Air Force Academy. So, by sheer luck and timing, I was awarded a pilot slot immediately following graduation and hence began my flying career.

I started my training at Columbus Air Force Base and was quickly made aware of how dangerous flying can be. First, because the planes we were flying were extremely old and second because of how demanding the flying was in the United States Air Force. At times, I questioned how any of this was safe, but as my knowledge of flying improved I realized that is what I was getting paid to do.

After my initial training, I was able to complete the second half of my training with the United States Navy. The culture of flying in the Navy is much different, but it was great to get different sides of aviation and certainly improved by overall knowledge of the world of aviation. I graduated from pilot training in May of 2001 and selected the EC-130H Compass Call as my aircraft. To complete my aircraft upgrade training in the C-130, I needed to attend the initial training program at Little Rock Air Force Base. Again, this was intense training that required proficient skills to become a good aircraft operator.

At this stage of training, the flying skills were already in place, so much of the focus was on emergency training. The simulator training focused on emergency procedures and this is really where I began to adopt a healthy fear of flying.

In the sims, we would run every possible situation you could get yourself into while flying a C-130. Often times, I would ask the instructors how often a certain malfunction occurs and many times the answer was "almost never." However, considering the age of the aircraft, I felt there was a good chance any of these malfunctions could occur during my time flying and the potential of this was always at the back of my mind.

Once completing my initial training at Little Rock Air Force Base, I was assigned to Davis-Monthan Air Force Base in Tucson, Arizona flying the EC-130H. These aircraft are unique as there are only 13 in the world and are used to support electronic warfare operations. They are also extremely old with multiple generations of modifications which led to a lot of maintenance complications. Furthermore, the mods to this aircraft created a massive amount of drag and increased the basic weight by almost 30 thousand pounds - neither of which is great for performance. This fact was quickly observed my first few months flying this aircraft as it was riddled with unique situations.

In my first year, I experienced 75% of the malfunctions my simulator instructors at Little Rock said would rarely happen. One particular failure was experienced while accomplishing proficiency training. The hydraulic system boost packs began to malfunction and started to give inputs to the control surfaces. This was a hairy situation and during landing, the aircraft tried to pitch up and roll to the right. It took all our strength to level the aircraft and get it on the ground. Our crew ended up winning the ACC Flight Safety Award for our actions. Unfortunately, on my very next flight, a different aircraft in the fleet did the same exact thing, although with less violent inputs from the hydraulic system. The fleet was grounded for several weeks while the problem was analyzed. As you can imagine, the crew wasn't very excited about flying these aircraft, but ultimately the problem was identified and we went back to flying.

In my time flying, I shutdown approximately 20 engines, experienced total electrical failure, multiple hydraulic failures, had a crew member get electrocuted, and countless other emergencies. The only emergency situation I didn't encounter was throttle control failure which is just a really bad day.

From these experiences, I developed a few informal rules that I constantly lived by while flying.

Lessons Learned:

1. Always keep a healthy fear: Flying an old aircraft made it easy to always be ready for a bad situation. After a while, I embraced the fact that I was flying old aircraft and wanted to be "the guy" that saves a crew when shit hits the fan. Never become so comfortable that you lose focus.

2. Learn the Regulations and Follow Them: This may sound obvious, but many pilots don't put enough effort into their craft. There is a lot to learn and you have to make it your business to always study and learn.

3. Trust what the plane is telling you: The EC-130H had many different indicators that would often fail erroneously, but it was

important to trust those gauges and not try to be smarter than the aircraft or the manuals.

4. Airspeed and Altitude are life: In the EC-130H, the heavy weight and excessive drag pushed the limits of the aircraft. During the summer, our 2-engine service ceiling was subterranean. During takeoff role I would always be aware of how quickly things could go wrong and be in a situation where there would be nothing I could do to save the crew and aircraft. I would focus all my attention on that first few many and always be ready to take immediate action if something went wrong.

5. In an emergency situation, ALWAYS focus on flying the plane first: Many high-profile aviation accidents occurred when pilots fixated on a problem instead of flying the aircraft. As an instructor and evaluator, we would always simulate emergencies during training missions. One thing I would tell my students was *"take a deep breath and analyze the situation, while still flying the aircraft and following the manual."* I've found pilots want to hurry up and handle the situation as quick as possible, but the best approach is to take your time and be methodical about handling the situation.

David Sheller
(Major, USAF, Retired)

Former Pilot and Assistant Director of Operations (including Chief of Safety), USAF. Currently Sales Manager GE Digital Solutions

INTRODUCTION
TOM HENRICKS

51 Lessons From The Sky is a life saver! Fletcher McKenzie's compilation of 51 U.S. Air Force pilot and maintainer experiences should be mandatory reading for every student pilot and all those talented professionals that keep flying machines flying.

Many of the lessons, the book actually contains more than 51, apply to life in general. Human actions and attitudes that prevent aircraft accidents can also prevent mistakes we make during our lives on the ground.

Having spent nearly five decades visiting the sky flying fighters, test piloting, orbiting in space, skydiving, and operating light aircraft, I truly love being in the sky. But I hate that dear friends and colleagues lost their lives in those activities. Lessons in this book could have saved most of them.

My own *lessons from the sky* began as a 19 year old parachuting instructor at the U. S. Air Force Academy. At the Academy, first jumps were ten second freefalls, no static line. As jumpmasters responsible for "pushing" other 19 year olds out of a plane at 3500 feet AGL, we told our students that if they experienced a parachute malfunction, they'd have the rest of their lives to resolve it. We told ourselves that if the student failed to learn, the instructor failed to teach. We never lost a student. The lessons that panic/inaction in the sky may be lethal, and that instructors of the sky must ensure their students "get it", are life-saving lessons.

Over the years, I have lost many friends and colleagues in accidents, including the two Space Shuttle accidents and the Thunderbirds formation accident in 1982. But, I learned the most from the New Years Day 1974 loss of my friend and classmate, "Bubba" Jones. While giving a neighbor a ride in his T-6, the engine failed and the aircraft impacted the ground in a nose low stall. Apparently, his non-pilot passenger held the stick full aft rather than letting Bubba make a controlled off runway landing. That accident instilled in me a lifelong respect for the dangers of flying and motivated me to learn as much as possible from others, my life's lessons from the sky.

In this book, no one dies...the objective of the book. Learn from others and fly safely!

Terence T. "Tom" Henricks
(Colonel, USAF, Retired)
NASA Astronaut (Former)

Henricks completed pilot training at Craig Air Force Base in Selma, Alabama, and F-4 conversion training at Homestead Air Force Base in Miami, Florida. He flew the F-4 in fighter squadrons in England and Iceland. After attending the USAF Test Pilot School in 1983, he was an F-16C test pilot and Chief of the 57th Fighter Weapons Wing Operating Location until his NASA selection in 1985. Henricks became an astronaut in July 1986 and was the commander of two Space Shuttle missions and the pilot of two others. He became the first person to log over 1,000 hours as a Space Shuttle pilot/commander. He has 749 parachute jumps and a Master Parachutist rating. He has flown 30 different types of aircraft, and logged over 6,000 hours flying time. He holds an FAA commercial pilot rating.

SPECIAL HONORS: The Distinguished Flying Cross, the NASA Outstanding Leadership Medal, the Defense Superior Service Medal, the Defense Meritorious Service Medal, two Air Force Meritorious Service Medals, two Air Force Commendation Medals, four NASA Space Flight Medals, Honorary Doctor of Science degree from the Defiance College (1993), F-4 Fighter Weapons School Outstanding Flying Award. Named Pilot Training Distinguished Graduate and F-16 Conversion Course Top Gun. Inducted into the Ohio Veterans Hall of Fame.[1]

---

1. https://www.jsc.nasa.gov/Bios/htmlbios/henricks.html

PROLOGUE
FLETCHER MCKENZIE

I have always been interested in military aircraft and the air forces of the world. They are complex organizations that live and breathe to support a select number of pilots. Their mission is to fly and to fly often - if not operational missions, then training missions to build best practice. On reflection, I enjoy that people can join an organization who pays you to learn, train and fly almost every day.

At the time of writing the United States Air Force (USAF) is the largest, most capable, and advanced air force in the world with 5,778 manned aircraft in service, 156 Unmanned Combat Air Vehicles, 2,130 Air-Launched Cruise Missiles, and 450 intercontinental ballistic missiles, including F-22 Raptors, F-35, F-15 and F-16 fighters. It operates B-2, B-1 and B-52 strategic bombers, and C-5, C-17 and C-130 airlift transporters. Operating from bases in the United States and around the world, the USAF manages everything from intercontinental ballistic missiles to X-37 space planes to A-10 Thunderbolt tank killers. It coordinates military space launches, airdrops of Army paratroopers and assists with mass relief efforts.

The USAF has one of the largest outdated fleets. With cost overruns and cutbacks, programs to replace the 1950s bomber and tanker fleets have commenced again after many aborted attempts. What the USAF can achieve with these outdated machines is a testament to the passionate men and women who serve in the USAF. The USAF comprises 328,439 personnel on active duty, 74,000 in Ready Reserves, and 106,000 in the Air National Guard, and employs 168,900 civilian personnel. That is 570,000 people engaged in an organization to achieve one mission, "Fly, Fight and Win - In Air, Space and Cyberspace." With a tagline of "We do the impossible every day".

The active duty personal number of the USAF comes in just behind the People's Liberation Army Air Force (China). As of 2014, the PLAAF had a strength of 398,000 and operates 2,755 to 3,010 aircraft. The USAF operates 3,000 more aircraft than the PLAAF. The Russian Air Force (a branch of the Russian Aerospace Forces formed on 1 August 2015 with the merger of the Russian Air Force and the Russian Aerospace Defense Forces) has 148,000 personnel (2018) and operates 3,200 aircraft.

To understand the number of people, look at other US companies and the number of staff employed. If the USAF were a company, it would rank #2 to Walmart. Walmart employs 2.3 million people, Amazon is #2 with 566,000, Accenture has 459,000 people and so on.

The first air force to fly stealth combat aircraft, to fly fifth-generation fighters, and to commit to an all-stealth combat aircraft force. The USAF are preserving this leading edge by purchasing 1,763 F-35s and up to 100 optionally manned Long-Range Strike Bombers. Unmanned aerial vehicles, increasingly with stealthy profiles and attack capabilities, will gradually represent a larger proportion of the overall aircraft fleet. They expect the all-in price to break US$1.1 trillion over the coming decades, high enough that it could force the Air Force to slash its aircraft orders by a full third.

The United States Air Force was born on 18 September 1947. Before this, US military aviation was divided between the Army for land-based aircraft operations and the Navy and Marine Corps for sea-based operations from aircraft carriers and amphibious aircraft. The Army created the first version of many versions of the Air Force on 1 August 1907 with the Aeronautical Division, Signal Corps. In 1914 this became the Aviation Section, Signal Corps, then in 1918 for only four days it was the Division of Military Aeronautics before becoming the Air Service, US Army until 1926. In 1926 it became the US Army Air Corps until 1941 when it became the US Army Air Forces. It stood alone as one organization in 1947 when the United States Air Force was incorporated.

Combined, the US Navy and Marine Corps are the world's second-largest air force, with over 3,700 aircraft. This includes 1,159 fighters, 133 attack aircraft, 172 patrol aircraft, 247 transports and 1,231 helicopters. The aircraft of the US Navy protect the US fleet and conducting air missions from and over the world's oceans and seas. Most of the aircraft of the Navy and Marine Corps operate from ships at sea, a difficult and dangerous job requiring a high level of training and proficiency.

As a boy I grew up with a large element of my fathers influence on me and I blame him for my passion for aviation after listening to his stories and facts on aircraft, the air forces, the airlines, World War Two fighters, the famous Spitfire, the legendary Hurricane and the infamous P-51 Mustang. Dad loved building things, including the house I grew up in. As a child, my father's family was not wealthy, my grandfather didn't own a car until he retired and as a family they often caught the bus. As a child, Dad used balsa-wood blocks to carve aircraft, by hand, and with no decals he hand painted his creations. I am lucky to still own Dad's models, with his British Hawker Hurricane on display in my office. He loved the Hurricane, and this year our television production company, Leading Edge Media, filmed a 1942 Hurricane, visiting the Temora Aviation Museum in New South Wales, Australia. I was rigging cameras in the Hurricanes' cockpit when the ground crew asked if I didn't mind the Hurricane being moved. No problem! They wheeled around the aircraft and I thought to myself there are very few people who can say they have been for a "ride" in a single seat WWII Hurricane.

For hours Dad and I watched the epic WWII movies: *Battle of Britain, The Dam Busters, Where Eagles Dare, The Bridge on the River Kwai, The Great Escape*, etc. The first American aircraft to attract my attention were the B-17 and the P-51. Two great examples of what and how an air force can dominate the skies.

One movie of great influence was *The Great Waldo Pepper* released in 1975. Set during 1926–1931, the film stars Robert Redford as a WWI veteran pilot. For me to see the frustration of the Great Waldo as an ex-WW1 pilot, who missed out on the glory of aerial combat, made me understand the yearning for the sky, to be free from gravity, to fly or dive or turn on any axis. Total freedom.

One movie changed everything for me - *The Right Stuff*, released in 1983. An inspiring story about test pilot pioneers, the astronauts and men who broke the sound barrier and walked on the moon. The Navy, Marine and Air Force test pilots who flew for the aeronautical research programme at Edwards Air Force Base, California, including the Mercury Seven - the seven military pilots selected to be the astronauts for Project Mercury, the first manned spaceflight by the United States. As a 13-year-old, I was spellbound - what a movie! The stories, the adventure, and from that moment, I wanted to join the air force.

In 1986, the movie *Top Gun* hit our screens. Although it showcased the US Navy and not the US Air Force, it contained the right balance of aviation - good vs evil. At the time, the Royal New Zealand Air Force ran recruiting ads in the cinemas, and their thunderous Skyhawks flew across the screen at my local theater before we even saw Tom Cruise, and I was hooked. Top Gun remains an awesome movie - with action and flying, a boyhood dream. Released during the height of the Cold War, *Top Gun's* plot revolved around the best of the best naval pilots training to be even better, with the climax seeing the US Navy taking on Russian Migs (F-5's painted black with red stars). I wanted to become an aviator, even saved up my money to buy a pair of Ray Ban aviators with mirrored lenses and a white Hanes T-shirt. I felt I was halfway there, I never took up volleyball, however...

Only forming as an Air Force in 1947, the USAF is the youngest branch of all the five services, but their roots are well over a hundred years old. Detailed below are a few air force legends who influenced my understanding of the global impact the USAF.

A self-taught pilot, Eddie Rickenbacker joined the military as soon as the United States entered WWI. Within twelve months he earned a promotion to an officer's rank and shot down his fifth enemy aircraft, gaining the title of "Ace." By wars end Rickenbacker recorded 26 aerial victories - a record held until WWII. His well-known tactic was to charge at enemy flying squadrons, no matter the odds, winning every time. He received the Distinguished Service Cross with six oak leaf clusters, the Croix de Guerre with two palms, the French Légion d'honneur, and later the Medal of Honor.

First Lieutenant "Bob" Hoover, is another. A United States Army Air Forces fighter pilot, USAF and civilian test pilot, flight instructor, air show pilot, aviation record-setter, he is a true aviation legend. I heard him speak at the media briefing at Oshkosh in 2011, wow, a treasure trove of information. He set transcontinental, time-to-climb, and speed records, and knew such great aviators as Orville Wright, Eddie Rickenbacker, Charles Lindbergh, Jimmy Doolittle, Chuck Yeager, Jacqueline Cochran, Neil Armstrong and Yuri Gagarin. Hoover is best known for his civil air show career, and for creating the stunt of pouring a cup of tea while performing a 1G barrel roll. You Tube has great footage of this famous stunt.

With an author for a wife, our home is filled with books, two of which I can recommend - *Lords of the Sky,* and *The Hunter Killers,* both written by Lieutenant Colonel Dan Hampton - outstanding books, well researched, containing great insight to military aviation advancement and the Wild Weasels and the role they played. Hampton is also the author of the New York Times bestseller *Viper Pilot: A Memoir of Air Combat.* He served with the US Air Force from 1986 to 2006, and flew 151 combat missions in the F-16, he was a "Wild Weasel", or Surface-to-Air (SAM) site killer, recording 21 kills on SAM sites. He fought in the Gulf War, Kosovo War and Iraq War.

In 2008, I attended a party in Washington DC, where I met Tom Henricks, the then President of Aviation Week - the leading information and media business serving the aerospace industry. A former NASA astronaut, Henricks flew four Space Shuttle missions as commander and pilot. The only astronaut assigned to Space Shuttle Program management during return to flight following the Challenger accident. Tom retired from the US Air Force as a colonel having served as a commander, F-16 test pilot, and F-4 fighter pilot. He is a graduate of the USAF Academy. We met again in the Aviation Week office in New York to discuss how Aviation Week could use more video content. While that meeting did not eventuate to any future work, I hoped to interview Tom and capture his stories for the world to see. While writing *51 Lessons From The Sky,* I reached out to Tom to write the introduction.

I met David Sheller at the 2018 C-130 TCG International Technical Program Review in Orlando. A chance encounter with the retired USAF major, turned into a discussion on the C-130, the military, and the realization that we were both passionate about all things aviation. I'd first flown in the RNZAF C-130 Hercules as a teenager, David gets to work with them all the time. I am honored that David agreed to write a piece for this book, to share his experiences.

With our High Definition TV show, *FlightPathTV*, we worked with the USAF Pacific Forces based in Hawaii and met several amazing USAF pilots. The Pacific Forces were most supportive of us filming positive stories, instead of disaster stories.

We started filming at the Australian International Airshow at Avalon, Australia in 2007, and it was this event where we first met with the USAF Public Relations team. I remember those early discussions with the USAF and the subsequent interview with experienced F-16 demo pilot Paul Miller. We filmed his interview in front of the F-16, with our PR escort alongside, and captured interesting facts and stories from him - being shot at and evading surface-to-air missiles's during his time in Bosnia (which reminded me of Scott O'Grady). I sat in the cockpit as Paul showed me the controls and I even experienced non-flying stick time - a different feeling with the side stick with only small inputs required.

WWII pilot Colonel Charlie Cook was 21-years-old when he flew the Boeing B-17 bomber - which became the birthplace for the first ever 'checklist' which is now just as important as the wings and control surfaces we need for flying. We met Charlie at Reno Air Races, he tells us how great the B-17 was and how stable despite losing most of their tail once... One of his stories included how all air crews had to drink one third a glass of scotch whisky upon landing, before the debrief. He kept saying how lucky he was surviving 35 bombing missions and had the honor of getting into the Lucky Bastards Club. His first B-17 was aptly named Lady Luck, named after a cafe he and his crew went to. He kept several napkins from the cafe and gave me one to keep. Despite being shot down twice, he never lost the desire to fly and flew often after the war.

We have been fortunate to film a number of stories with the USAF including climbing all over the infamous B-52. I remember stopping to ask what a box I noticed was for, with the chilling reply that it was the box for the nuclear launches. We filmed the heavy lifter C-5 Galaxy and heard how they carried one of the famous Shamu (Orca - killer whale) from Sea World.

Another highlight was accessing the cockpit of the Boeing B-1B Bone, meant to serve as the replacement for the B-52 Bomber. We interviewed 28-year-old Captain David Grasso from the 37th Bomb Squadron. David gave us a great understanding of the B-1B role and then told us about how out of his 68 missions, the scariest one was when he got hit by lightning and lost electronics for a period. He finishes his story with how he loves to fly the B-1B but, more importantly, he gets to serve his country.

Being able interview the F-22 demo team was a highlight.

Australian aviation photographer, Michael Jorgensen, took photographs of us interviewing the crew, one of which appeared on the front page of the Pacific Wings magazine. The photo didn't show the USAF security behind us and the two Australian Military Police with their German Shepherd's... At one stage, when positioning for the photo's, we got too near to the aircraft, and they firmly told us to step away from the F-22.

The biggest highlight for me as a pilot was flying the F-35 simulator, a mind-bending experience with the 5th generation helmet. Imagine flying and looking through your own body, through the aircraft, to the outside world? The systems were easy to use, like a big iPhone.

One ex USAF pilot I met was Colonel Raynor Roberts from Montana. The then 88-year-old surprised us while we were filming Air Force One (tail number 27000) - a Boeing 707, at The Ronald Reagan Presidential Library in Simi Valley, California. He happened to be visiting to see Air Force One as he had piloted the aircraft. He was also a WWII fighter pilot, flying over 70 combat missions and shot down numerous enemy aircraft. He flew on D-Day and in the Korean War and recounted stories from his WWII encounters and his Air Force One days flying the Kennedy's and President Johnson. An amazing look through the historic window of his life, and for that I am truly grateful.

I read many stories from the US Air Force Safety Center, and picked out 51 that I believe most pilots, either military, aerobatic, commercial or even private, will learn from.

The majority of the stories in these pages are longer than those in my Air Transport book - *101 Lessons From The Sky*, although I also included a few interesting short stories taken from the "Aviation Well Done Awards", inspiring stories that make you sit and think, what would I do?

The next few hundred pages contain stories of the men and women of the US Air Force. Read, learn and make notes because as Buzz Aldrin said, "Keep in mind that progress is not always linear. It takes constant course correcting and often a lot of zigzagging. Unfortunate things happen, accidents occur, and setbacks are usually painful, but that does not mean we quit."

Enjoy learning from the stories as I did.

Fletcher McKenzie

HOW TO USE THIS BOOK

A glossary of terms is included at the end of this book for your reference. Please note that this book may contain a mixture of both American English and British English, depending on who is telling the story.

If you find a term or an acronym in this book which isn't in the glossary, please email Fletcher:

fletch@avgasgroup.com

Each lesson includes space for you to make your own notes if you want to. I recommend doing this to cement the learning.

Writing a short review of this book on Amazon, BookBub, Goodreads, or on your personal blog or Facebook page, will help spread the word about aviation safety. Saving lives is the primary goal of this book.

US AIR FORCE AVIATION SAFETY

The Air Force Safety Center resides on Kirtland Air Force Base, located in the high desert of north-central New Mexico and it occupies a majority of southeast Albuquerque.

The Aviation Safety Division (SEF) consists of safety-trained professionals spanning the domain of flight. The division preserves warfighting capability by establishing Air Force aviation safety policy, promoting mishap prevention programs for all aviation assets and through the establishment of proactive safety programs.

It oversees the aviation mishap investigative process, the collection and accuracy of flight safety data and the disposition of risk-mitigating actions. It provides proactive and reactive engineering and operational analyses of flight safety issues.

Additionally, the division directs the Aircraft Information Program, the Hazardous Air Traffic Report Program, the Bird Aircraft Strike Hazard Program and the Mishap Analysis and Animation Facility.

How Aviation Safety became to what it is today.

In the 1950s when the Air Force became a separate department, the Air Force Chief of Staff designated the Office of the Inspector General to oversee all inspection and safety functions. These functions were consolidated in an inspector general group at Norton Air Force Base, California.

On Dec. 31, 1971, the Air Force Inspection and Safety Center was activated, replacing the 1002nd Inspector General Group. The center was then divided into the Air Force Inspection Agency and the Air Force Safety Agency in August 1991. Reorganization of the air staff in 1992 created the Air Force Chief of Safety position, reporting directly to the Air Force Chief of Staff. The Chief of Safety became dual-hatted as the commander of the Air Force Safety Agency. In July 1993, the agency moved to Kirtland Air Force Base due to the closure of Norton Air Force Base.

Following The Blue Ribbon Panel on Aviation Safety in 1995, the Air Force Safety Center was activated on Jan. 1, 1996, when the Air Force Chief of Safety and support staff moved from Washington, D.C., to consolidate all safety functions at Kirtland Air Force Base. The Chief of Safety position was changed from a brigadier general to a major general.

The Deputy Chief of Safety/Executive Director position was created in October 2003 to oversee the daily functions of the center. The Chief of Safety and support staff moved back to the Pentagon in April 2004.

The Air Force Chief of Safety, who also holds the title of commander, Air Force Safety Center, heads the organization and is located at the Pentagon with an Air Staff liaison division. The Air Force Safety Center is composed of the Deputy Chief of Safety/Executive Director and 10 divisions at its Kirtland Air Force Base location.

CHAPTER 1
PREPARATION & PLANNING

"We need to try to do the right thing every time, to perform at our best, because we never know which moment in our lives we'll be judged on."

Captain Chesley B. Sullenberger, USAF

WAKE TURBULENCE
C-130E, 43RD AIRLIFT WING, POPE AFB, N.C.

Captain David Kegerreis, Oct 2008

It had been three long months in the desert; 18-hour crew duty days; often staying awake for 24 hours at a time. I often found myself flying the final approach with fatigue equivalent to a blood alcohol content of between .05 and point one. But, that was not the case this day. This day was supposed to be easy. It was the final leg of the 6,500 mile journey from the desert back to Pope Air Force Base, N.C. We woke up around 10 a.m. after an excellent night's sleep. Takeoff was at 2 p.m. with a four-ship formation from Providence, R.I. to Pope. It was a simple high-level formation with 4,000 feet between our C-130Es.

About 20 miles from Pope, we dropped down to 500 feet AGL and closed up to visual formation position (1,000 to 2,000 feet in trail). We were No. 3, got long, and had to accelerate to 270 indicated to gain position. We were to do a 500-foot overhead, breaking with a sixty-and-two over Pope's Green Ramp where families, friends and media were eagerly awaiting our return from Operation Iraqi Freedom. It would be spectacular. I vividly remember the flags waving, large welcome home banners, the news trucks with cameras rolling, and all the husbands, wives and children waiting for their loved ones to come home.

Lead broke at the appointed spot that would bring his aircraft directly over the cheering crowd. No. 2 broke and followed lead. One potato, two potato, and I smoothly began to roll into 60 degrees of coordinated bank, brought the power to flight idle, and added back pressure to maintain altitude. But the plane didn't stop at 60 degrees; it continued to roll past 60 — "bank angle," — to 70, 80 — "bank angle," — 90 degrees, and then some. I slammed the yoke to the left and held on with all I had. I kept the throttles at flight idle since we were already doing 250 knots. The nose dropped, and this was where I got the best aerial view of green ramp I'd ever seen. I actually had time to pick out the place we were going to impact.

It seemed like an eternity, but it was only a second or two before the ailerons become effective again and the plane began to waffle out of its extreme bank angle. We had lost 200 feet of altitude before we fully recovered.

We rolled out to 30 degrees of bank and then back to 60 as we climbed up and attempted to regain formation position. We configured on the downwind and landed uneventfully. More than one crew member was still shaking as we taxied to park. The question on everybody's lips was, "What the heck was that all about?" Two words — wake turbulence. Some witnesses on the ground thought we were showing off, as did my squadron commander. "No, sir, that was wake turbulence trying to flip us over and crash us into a crowd of unsuspecting onlookers. Nice to see you again."

Despite its dangers, wake turbulence accounts for a surprisingly low number of aircraft mishaps. However, we want our low numbers even lower. Reducing that number to zero is the goal. Here is a quick review of the standard rules for avoiding wake turbulence. See Figure 1.

Figure 1

Digital illustration by Felicia M. Hall

- Wait three minutes to land after a "heavy" aircraft departs or lands
- Wait one minute behind like aircraft
- Rotate before the previous plane's rotate point and stay above its path
- On final, fly "one dot" above the preceding aircraft's glide slope
- Land beyond the previous plane's touchdown point
- Pass above and well behind crossing traffic, one mile or more if able
- Wake turbulence dissipates quicker with strong crosswinds and lingers with light winds

Those rules tend to work for taking off, landing or flying around by yourself. What about taking off and flying in formation? Aside from Large Package Week at Pope Air Force Base, it's perhaps the most dangerous thing we do in the mighty Hercules. For example, as a young co-pilot during one formation pass over Sicily drop zone, I found my plane loaded with 55 airborne troopers caught up in lead's wake turbulence. In retrospect, I'm pretty glad that I wasn't flying. Even with the pilot applying max power, full aileron and full rudder, our plane continued to slip and rock violently, but he somehow managed to keep the plane pretty much upright. The loadmaster reported a jumper exiting the aircraft and actually coming back in before bouncing out again. It was ugly. During a formation takeoff earlier, I witnessed No. 2 get pushed directly to the right, obviously struggling to regain aircraft control and spraying fuel from the right wing tip. I remember thinking those guys must have soiled their pants during that maneuver. Yet we continue to fly in formation. So what can we do to mitigate the risks associated with this invisible killer we call wake turbulence? We may already be doing all we can, but revisiting this potentially deadly phenomenon just might give you the tools needed to recognize, avoid or get out of it.

Starting with a quick review of wake vortices' characteristics may help. Wake turbulence is caused by the lift, creating high pressure under the wing rapidly moving over the wing tip to the low pressure area on top. This causes tornado like vortices to flow from the wing tips. The characteristics are more pronounced when the aircraft is heavy, slow and clean, thus generating the most lift, i.e., after cleaning up during takeoff. The vortices move clockwise off the left wing tip and counterclockwise from the right when viewed from behind. They typically fall down and away from the aircraft.

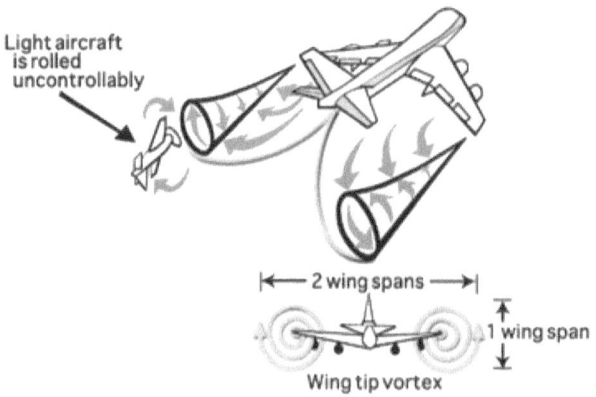

Digital illustration by Felicia M. Hall

Let's go over what else we know and why this is such a serious problem for C-130 aircraft. We know that below 125 knots indicated, the C-130 may not have the aileron authority to overcome the effects of wake turbulence generated by a preceding C-130. We also know that drop airspeed for personnel is 130 knots. Most C-130 pilots typically brief they'll maintain plus or minus five knots on airspeed, so that doesn't leave much of a buffer for a potential wake turbulence encounter during a drop.

Moreover, we take off with a 15-second interval, not the two minutes or more that is recommended by the FAA, and our rotate airspeeds are typically not much higher than 100 knots. This is when we're most vulnerable. Here is an account from my buddy on his first formation takeoff without an instructor and only his third flight as an aircraft commander.

> "We departed as the second aircraft of a two-ship formation. Takeoff speed was 109 kts. Passing 200 feet, we flew into lead's wake turbulence. The aircraft began roll off to the left. I applied max power and full right aileron, but we were now rolling through 30 degrees of left bank at 110 kts. At that point, there wasn't much more I could do but stay coordinated and ride it out. We were too slow to pull the nose up and climb through the vortices, too low to let it drop and build up some speed. Eventually, we got spit out of the turbulence, regained full control and continued the departure for an uneventful afternoon of dropping 18 ABN paratroopers."

So what really happened? The C-130E(H)-1 states, "The forces from C-130 wing tip vortices can easily exceed the aileron authority of a following C-130 at 125 kts" (page 6-5). This was a formation departure, so they were 15 seconds behind the lead aircraft. It's right there in black and white. If you find yourself in wake turbulence below 125 kts, you can expect little or no aileron authority. We do that every day. The situation described above was aggravated because the wake turbulence caused the aircraft to roll into a 30-degree bank. At that particular takeoff gross weight, power-off stall speed at 30 degrees was 101 kts. If they had continued to roll to 45 degrees of bank, the stall speed would have been 113 kts — three knots below their current speed. Thankfully, they exited the vortices before rolling any further.

Up to this point, I haven't offered many solutions in the way of correcting the dangers inherent in the C-130 mission. I'm not here to change the way we've done things for decades; however, here are a few things that should be considered and thoroughly briefed before "stepping to the jet" for a seemingly routine trip around yellow route for a personnel drop at Luzon DZ.

Let's start with the takeoff. We've already discussed the 15-second takeoff interval. Imperative to our mission is getting into formation position, so extending the takeoff interval is impractical. However, we can use our favorite wake turbulence techniques to keep ourselves out of trouble. A good technique would be for lead to momentarily delay his rotation, perhaps to 125 knots, and shallow out his climb. This will allow his wingmen to rotate before and climb above lead's flight path. In a crosswind situation, a good idea is to manoeuvre upwind of the preceding aircraft's flight path to decrease the likelihood of passing through his wake vortices. In calm winds, manoeuvre slightly left or right as appropriate to avoid the turbulence. Worry about getting in position once you've gotten away from the ground.

Now that we've successfully avoided our preceding aircraft's wing tip tornados on takeoff, let's discuss the drop. Intuitively, stacking each plane 50 feet sounds like a good idea, but it's not practical for large formations. It's slightly effective when we stack multiple element formations (three-ships), but isn't much help to the guys behind their element leader. During high-drift situations, we automatically set ourselves up to avoid wake turbulence with our angled track into the drop zone, but during light winds, we're 2,000 feet directly behind lead. Since we're dropping visually, it seems reasonable to move slightly upwind and accept a deviation in our drop score. At some point, though, we're going to run out of drop zone and be stuck behind lead. Now what? Tragically, we sit back and hope we don't get caught in wake turbulence. If we do get caught, we've hopefully armed ourselves with the tools to get out. Section six of our dash one describes the recovery procedure. At the first indication of encountering wake turbulence, "[Warning] Immediate application of maximum power and maximum coordinated deflection of flight controls may be required to exit the wake turbulence. Elevator back pressure may be necessary to minimize altitude loss." You may want to brief your engineer to close the bleed air valves upon encountering wake turbulence. Every bit of power will aid in a successful recovery.

Lessons Learned:

Having a good plan is essential. We haven't fundamentally changed the way we fly formation since before I was born, and it isn't likely that it'll change any time soon. Bring it up to any "old hat" and he or she will tell you, "That's the way we've always done it."

This attitude, my friends in flight, is an entirely different safety issue all together. For now, realize that the nature of formation operations — especially C-130 formations — puts us in the wake turbulence envelope from takeoff through landing. Admittedly, it's a manageable risk. Your experiences and skills as pilots will also be called into play.

You should always do everything you can to avoid wake turbulence, but if you can't avoid it, at least apply max power and stay coordinated. Abrupt rudder inputs or high rudder deflections at high power/low airspeed can cause a fin stall to develop, and now your day just got a whole lot worse.

Keep the ball centered, and no matter what — keep flying.

NOTES:

THERE I WAS...
C-17, TRANSPORT, AIR ARMAMENT CENTER, EGLIN AFB, FLA.

Lt. Col. Joel Witte, September 2008

There I was (a fairly long time ago) flying the C-17 out in the system back before deployments, back when Prince Sultan Air Base and Northern/Southern Watch were still around. My crew and I deadheaded from the states to Ramstein to pick up a used-to-be-broke C-17 to be followed by a cargo/ pax pickup in Egypt and return to the states. When we arrived, the bird was still broke, well, sort of. It had a fuel leak in one of its Aux tanks. With waiver in hand, TACC pushed us from Ramstein to Rhein Mein for fuel cell maintenance. Not a bad trade: Egypt for Frankfurt. We got fixed and expected to be on our way home. No chance — we got picked to take our newly fixed "good" bird down to Rota NAS, Spain and give it to another crew who had been stuck with a bad jet for several days. Again, not bad, spend some time in Spain and then go home. Well, this is where my story really starts.

Hangar flying is one of those sometimes lost, sometimes profound lessons that proved it's worth its weight in gold on this trip, plus it's a lot easier to think about a situation at 1G and 0 knots. When we arrived at Rota, we gave our jet to the crew that was waiting to go downrange to Kuwait and went into crew rest. After a few ZZZs, I was wandering the halls at billeting and ran into the aircraft commander who had supposedly taken my aircraft. He related that they didn't get very far before having a problem. Twenty minutes into climb out, one of the two fire bottles on the right wing indicated that it had depressurized. The crew discussed the issue and decided it was wise to RTB to Rota and try to get it fixed, since flying around with less than the prescribed safety equipment seemed to be a bad idea.

Maintenance came out to the jet, determined that the empty bottle was probably caused by a bleed air leak directly on the fire bottle, resulting in the pressure relief squib letting go and releasing the extinguishing agent inside the wing. But, by the time the bottle could be replaced and the suspected loose bleed air fitting could be tightened, the crew had long run out of crew duty day to complete the mission. Then he told me that TACC was probably going to alert my crew for the mission at the conclusion of our crew rest. Woohoo! Didn't think we were going to be anywhere near that part of the sandbox on this trip nor collect any hostile fire pay or tax free. Sounded good to me.

Now, knowing that I'd be doing what he just tried to do, given the same scenario, I asked if he and his crew would have done anything differently?

He thought about it for a little bit and passed on some good points:

> 1. The decision to RTB with less than a full set of fire bottles was a good idea — you never know when Murphy's law will catch up with you. The C-17 has four fire bottles, two per wing, giving the crew a chance to fight an engine fire on each wing with two blasts of agent. The bottles cannot be used cross wing; therefore, with one bottle gone, there's only one bottle left for engines 3 and 4.

2. What caused the bottle to let go? The bottle is protected from thermal expansion by a diaphragm that relieves pressure when the agent's temperature exceeds 205 degrees C. How did it get that hot? Might suspect fire, bleed air leak or just a faulty diaphragm or indicator. The Manifold Failure Detection System didn't indicate any type of bleed air leak failure.

3. The fire bottle had to get hot somehow. Take away any potential source of heat if you don't need it. In other words, given the opportunity again, he would have just isolated the right wing bleed air manifold. This all sounded reasonable enough to me and with thoughts of how much beer this unexpected trip was going to buy me, I left him to his crew rest and prepared for my mission.

Takeoff out of Rota was uneventful. Past Sigonella, hang a right over Egypt, cross over Saudi Arabia and turn north into Kuwait. No problems at all. Offload some pallets, onload some pallets, fire the jet back up and take off from Kuwait.

Then I had déjà vu! About 20 minutes into flight we got the Agent A Low light on the right wing, just like the previous crew did. There was no Chapter 3 emergency procedure for fire bottles inexplicably discharging in flight and as of 2007, there still wasn't. Thinking back to my earlier conversation, I reached up and isolated the right wing manifold. It was dark, but the weather was clear, and I had no immediate concerns about icing. I knew we could stay pressurized with just the left wing manifold, so no worries there, either. We decided to level off at about FL200 and come up with a game plan. The loadmaster scanned the right wing, but could see little in the dark.

We decided there were three options at this point: divert to Prince Sultan Air Base in Saudi Arabia where we knew we could get maintenance; continue along our route and divert into Sigonella and get maintenance; or turn around and land back at Kuwait and wait for the maintenance repair team.

First, we tried PSAB, but the Saudis wouldn't let us land there without diplomatic clearances, unless we used the "E" word. Well, I wasn't quite sure that this required declaring an emergency, so we talked about making it to Sigonella, another 3½-hour flight from where we were, and I again went back to the hangar flying that we did earlier. Flying around for significant periods of time without all the safety equipment just didn't pass the good judgment test for me. One option remained: RTB Kuwait. A half hour later, we were uneventfully on the ground and had taxied to park. The loadmaster did a quick inspection of the right wing, and before I was even out of my seat, he was saying I had something to come look at. An eight-foot long panel on the lower skin of the right wing was swinging in the breeze — with a softball-sized hole in the middle of it. The fire bottle had not just discharged by outgassing through a thermal diaphragm this time; it had violently blown its connective ducting down through the bottom of the wing. Flying around with holes in the wing isn't the most comfortable feeling in the world. It was at that point that I was really glad I had made the decisions I had.

Multiple parts had to be replaced, to include the bleed air ducting that had ruptured, the fire bottle and its plumbing, and the lower wing access door. It cost us an extra week in Kuwait, but who knows what it could have cost us if it weren't for taking the time to talk about an unusual malfunction and what to do about it.

Lessons Learned:

Hangar flying is worth its weight in gold.

NOTES:

KEEP THE BRIEF SACRED

T-6, OPERATIONAL INFORMATION WITHHELD

Name withheld by request, August 2008

I had been a flight commander for about eight months, and had a pretty good feel for the job. I had also come to know the time crunch that occurs just before briefing a sortie. Everyone needs you to weigh in on something: "Can I fly this IP with that student?" "Can you sign off on my ORM?" The possibilities go on.

When I was simply a line IP, there were almost zero interruptions. You were essentially off on your own with your student. I know that it sounds like we don't keep the brief "sacred" in the SUPT environment. Every effort is made to do so, but due to the daily time crunch, some briefs start late and others are sometimes interrupted. Flight CCs and flight schedulers are the ones most often affected.

My brief started late, and we were interrupted, due the CAP status of a student and the IP requirements that are stipulated as part of the plan to get him off CAP. This was my student's first aerobatic ride. He'll perform a normal contact profile with the addition of an aileron roll, a loop and a split S. After the motherhood, I brief specifics on the aero. The words that come out of my mouth and seal the fate of my impending over-G are something to the effect of, "Classically speaking, most students don't pull enough G as they attempt to go over the top in the loop. You want to get on the G quickly and hold that 3-4 G pull." In a normal brief, following my statement concerning quickly getting on the G, I would make some reference to respecting the ops limits and not "snatching" the stick; however, this was one instance where the brief was interrupted. Some question was asked, I answered the question, the interrupting party left, and I commenced the brief. My memory wasn't perfect; however, I think all of the stars aligned, and I went right into the explanation of a split-S, without ever referencing the caution on "snatching" the stick and over-G'ing the aircraft. Looking back, that demonstrated lesson number one: never allow anyone to interrupt your brief. It's a slippery slope. And for the rest of your time flying with them, they'll always think it's OK.

After the step brief, we go to life support, taxi out, take off, hit the MOA, run through a standard contact profile, and then are set to start in on the aero. Part of the SUPT instruction business is adequately assessing the abilities of your student. In mixed company, I'd never say that you put each one of them into a predetermined container, but you do. You have the "ultra-intelligent, yet ultra-timid" container, the "x-airline pilot/F-16 guard slot/golden hands" container, and lastly the "watch-out-for-this-guy" container.

The student I was flying with this day had a military aviation-related background. His dad had flown for 20 years in the Navy. He listened closely to what you said, and did exactly what he thought you wanted him to do. He would've fallen into the "take-orders-and-don't-ask-questions" container. This is where lesson number two comes in: always keep the student's outlook and the way he's going to react to what you say in the back of your mind. This guy was a loaded gun when I gave him only half of the brief on how to fly a loop in this aircraft. Now if I had been flying with a student from the "ultra-intelligent/ultra-timid" container, nothing probably would've happened.

This was essentially the second link in the chain — I didn't have adequate SA on what this guy was capable of.

Back to the flight. The student performed a good G exercise and pulled in the neighborhood of 4.4 Gs. He had experience in the aircraft. I had given him a nice demo. I pulled 3.7 Gs on my loop. Now it was his turn. So this was the beautiful moment when he asked, "All right Sir, are you ready for this?" My mental reply was, "Of course I'm ready for this. This is a loop — how crazy can it be?" But at the same time, the way he questioned my readiness caught my attention. I sat up in the seat, got adjusted, and positioned my hands behind the stick. The phrase "Be ready for anything" came to mind. After the preparation, I replied, "Yeah dude, I'm ready; let's go." Little did I know that this guy had been warming up his biceps in the front seat for the quickest and deepest pull in history. He reefed back to 7.68 Gs for 1/16th of a second. He is a relatively thick, tough guy, and for all that I was worth, I couldn't stop him from pulling as hard as he did. The symmetric limit for the T-6 is 7 Gs. However, due to some questionable wing longerons, our limit had been temporarily dropped to 5.5 Gs. My meter in the back showed 7.1 Gs and his showed 6.5 Gs. By my meter, we had over G'ed by 1.6.

Discrepancies are pretty common due to the fore and aft position of the G meters, and MX won't adjust as long as the pulls are within 1.0 Gs of each other. The G meter associated with the data recorder is even further aft in the aircraft. That partly explained the different readings. (It would be nice if the tolerances were tightened up a bit.) If this SP had been solo after the limit had been returned to 7.0 Gs, he could've pulled his 6.5 Gs and actually registered 7.68 Gs on the data recorder. He would've over G'ed, cleared his meter, RTB'ed and never would've known anything wrong had happened.

Back to the flight and the third lesson: the guy essentially told me that he was going to over-G the aircraft right before he did it. He said, "All right, Sir, are you ready for this?" What he was actually saying was, "I've never done this before, but I'm about to expand my personal envelope of experience, and you'd better have your game face on." This is the point where I could've briefed him on the possible dangers and averted the situation. I hadn't, however, put together the pieces of the puzzle that were in 1/16th of a second going to become blatantly obvious.

It was my boss's words a couple weeks later when he was talking about students that brought all of this to mind. He said, "Right before the student tries to kill you, he'll tell you that he's going to do it." I thought back to every "dangerous" student situation that I've ever seen, and knew he was right. That student gave me the heads up that he was venturing into what for him was the great unknown.

Lessons Learned:

Keep the brief sacred, know the dude who you're flying with, and most importantly, listen not only to what the guy is saying, but also to what the guy is trying to convey.

NOTES:

AIRCRAFT STRIKE HAZARD
C-12J HURON, 459 AS YOKOTA AB, JAPAN

Captain Troy Saechao, May 2008

In the summer of 2007, I PCS'd to Yokota Air Base, Japan, as one of the C-12's initial cadre. The C-12J Huron arrived in Yokota to replace the C-21A. Before the move, the C-12 had been a part of the 55th Airlift Flight, Osan Air Base, Korea. The unit closed, and three pilots, including me, received orders to PCS from Osan to Yokota to help stand up the C-12s in its new unit, the 459th Airlift Squadron.

In addition to receiving the new aircraft, the squadron would also pick up the C-12's annual deployment, Operation Enduring Freedom-Philippines. The OEF-P mission supported the Global War on Terrorism by assisting the Philippine military deal with insurgents and terrorist organizations throughout the Philippine Islands.

Beginning in late August 2007, this deployment was the first for the Yokota C-12s, and it soon became a top priority for the squadron. "The aircraft just arrived here on July 1 and started flying missions in August, making this a pretty quick stand up for a deployment," said Lt. Col. Sara Beyer, squadron director of operations (Summers, 2007).

As the initial OEF-P mission commander, I had about one month to plan and prepare for the deployment. Although I had no experience with OEF-P, I knew there was a lot to do from all the stories and advice I received from the 55 ALF pilots who had participated in the previous year's deployment.

Items on the to-do list included a study of the Philippine airfields and request for waivers to operate on some of these fields. Airfields required a waiver if they were not in the Airfield Suitability and Restrictions Report or didn't meet minimum C-12J runway width and length requirements.

Many airfields required a waiver. In particular, Jolo Airfield received special attention due to its runway length, condition and hazards. The runway needed a waiver because of its 4,000-foot length. It barely met minimum runway width (60 feet) and didn't have the greatest surface condition. While the field is included in the ASRR, the report didn't specify C-12 suitability. Furthermore, the field is day and visual flight rules only, due to no navigational aids, instrument approaches and runway lighting at the airport. In addition, takeoff and landing data prevented us from operating into this field with a wet runway. Finally, probably the most important factor is the number of hazards that existed on the field. At one end of the runway, trees and mountainous terrain allowed us to land and takeoff in only one direction and hampered the aircraft's go-around capability. Random foreign object damage and animals, such as stray dogs, would somehow make their way onto the runway and posed a tremendous risk. One of the more popular stories told to me by a 55 ALF pilot occurred during a takeoff at Jolo. The pilots had passed the go/no-go decision speed, then saw a dog run onto the runway. Upon rotation, they heard a thump and continued to their next destination. After accomplishing a safe landing, they saw one of its landing gears covered in blood and guts. The U.S. Special Forces at Jolo later called to confirm that the poor dog was split in two.

Throughout the planning process and after taking all of these issues into consideration, I remember asking myself, "Do we really need to operate into this field?" The answer was, "Yes," as a huge part of the operation took place in Jolo.

Once the waivers were approved, we were legal to operate into the field. The Army and Navy also operated their C-12s into the field, and they assured me that it was not that bad. Of course, their model of the C-12 was smaller, and they operated under different rules compared to the Air Force. Moreover, if previous Air Force C-12J deployments operated into Jolo, then surely we could, right? Since this was the case, I was going to make sure that everything was accomplished to make operating at this field as safe as possible. Mitigating the risks became one of my top priorities in the planning process.

Before our deployment, crews practiced short-field landings in a new training program designed specifically for landing at Jolo. Aside from an airfield study, this was the best we could do in preparing for operations into the field. Unfortunately, there were no BASH plans or wildlife control. Even NOTAMs didn't have Jolo in its listings. I admit that I departed for the OEF-P deployment a little apprehensive about operating into that airfield.

The first time I flew into Jolo went as expected. The field was uncontrolled, and a quasi-fixed base operator asked over the radios if there were any aircraft currently operating at the field. Being a VFR-only field with no navaids or instrument approaches made finding the runway difficult at first. We relied solely on our eyes and terrain charts, not as common in the C-12 compared to other aircraft. Once we found the field, we accomplished a straight-in on the initial approach and performed a go-around to check the condition of the runway. Due to the obstacles at the departure end, we couldn't fly as low as we would have liked. To our best judgment, the runway looked clear, so we proceeded for another visual approach to land.

The narrow runway made landing on centerline critical. Upon touchdown, I noticed the runway condition. It was rough, and I could definitely feel the nose gear bounce up and down as we proceeded down the runway. Getting the aircraft to stop within the runway length was not a factor. However, what we saw at the end of the runway came as a surprise.

A wooden beam with a metal pole attached to it was just left of centerline. Three dogs had also found a nice resting spot in the middle of the runway. I couldn't imagine what would have happened if those items had been within our landing stopping distance. We stopped and accomplished the engine running off/onload checklist. I exited the aircraft to clear the beam from the runway and chase the dogs away. After returning to the plane, we started the engine to continue taxiing to the end. From there, we accomplished a 180-degree turn and accomplished another ERO to load the cargo. While loading the cargo, I noticed the dogs on the runway again. I asked the U.S. Special Forces soldier if he could clear the animals from the runway. When he began throwing rocks at them, I approached him again to clarify what I had meant. After the rocks and dogs were removed, we took off and completed the rest of the mission uneventfully.

My first experience at Jolo paved the way for how I wanted to operate into the field for the remainder of the deployment. From that point forward, crews flew a low approach before landing at the field. Every time Jolo was on the schedule, I also coordinated for U.S. Special Forces to clear the runway. For the most part, this was effective, and we operated for the remainder of the deployment without any mishaps or damage. Unfortunately, there were moments when Special Forces were unavailable and on those days, we never knew what we would see at Jolo. Throughout the course, we encountered livestock, a jogger, and children on the runway. Sometimes all on the same day. Luckily, no incidents ever came of it. When asked to describe the airfield, one of the pilots on the deployment replied, "There's no tower. There's no requesting to land. There's just a cow and a windsock" (Dubee, 2008).

Lessons Learned:

What I learned from this was twofold.

First, preparation plays a huge factor in mitigating risks. In this example, reviewing the airfields, practicing short-field landings, and sharing experiences from previous pilots all played a role in making me feel more comfortable about operating at the field. I would later use this during the crew swap and for ensuring a good handover for my replacements. I had Jolo scheduled for the swapout crew's first mission and even flew with them, discussing and pointing out the hazards.

The second concept I learned deals with the role of adaptability in the safety process. Since I had little knowledge and experience, I used my first trip to Jolo to help come up with a plan. As new situations arose, I learned to adapt and make changes to how we operated in and out of the field.

Clearing the runways and coordinating with the Special Forces on the ground are prime examples.

In the end, ensuring safety is a continuous, ever-changing process.

That's why safety programs exist today.

NOTES:

ELECTROSTATIC DISCHARGE
U-28A, SPECIAL OPERATIONS SQUADRON

Name withheld by request, Winter 2012

As a young captain, I was deployed to Operation Enduring Freedom, flying the new U-28A. The typical Afghanistan weather for summer to early winter is categorized by high winds during the day and sporadic thunderstorms in the late afternoon. This is locally referred to as the 120 Days of Wind.

I sat one night as the co-pilot to one of my instructors on a simple mission from Point A to B. There were a few puffies along our intended route, but no major weather phenomenon on the radar. We flew at 24,000 feet over a large mountain chain and stayed well clear of any clouds or possible storms. Flying with our night vision goggles, we saw an inordinate amount of static discharge and some intermittent St. Elmo's fire, despite staying clear of any thunderstorm activity. Sitting in the proverbial state of fat, dumb and happy, I didn't think too much about the current weather.

All of a sudden ... BAM! The plane felt like it hit severe turbulence. The pilot and I were thrown up and forward in our seats; our heads hit the top of the aircraft and knocked off our NVGs. The cockpit went completely dark, and the communication system failed. We looked at each other, then toward the back to confirm the passengers were OK. While obviously startled, the men wearing seatbelts were fine. The only one not wearing his seatbelt quickly remedied the situation, no worse for wear. The electrical system quickly came back online and restored power to our navigation and communication systems. After a quick check of all our systems and stability, we surmised that we must have been hit by lightning, but that we would be able to safely fly home to finish the mission. With no suitable place to land within 60 nautical miles, it was our only real option. The plane was quiet again, and I continued an impromptu functional check flight. Then we encountered our next potential problem. While advancing and retarding the throttle, we heard and felt the engine whine and shutter slightly. Despite my concerns, the rest of the mission proceeded uneventfully. We flew the remaining 50 nautical miles back to our destination and shut down.

We debriefed with the pilot and maintenance, then checked every square inch of the plane for external damage. We couldn't find any sign of damage.

I hit the books soon after to find an explanation for what could have happened. Our initial guess of a lightning strike may well have been an electrostatic discharge. Air Force Handbook 11-203, Vol. 1, Weather for Aircrews, described everything we encountered and the weather to match. Electrostatic discharges are very similar in most respects to lightning, with one exception. These are caused by the aircraft itself. Charges build up on the aircraft when flying through any form of precipitation, dust or even turbulence. The aircraft's electrical field then interacts with charged areas of the atmosphere, resulting in a discharge. After further discussion, and the lack of evidence of an actual lightning strike, we decided that we had, indeed, encountered an electrostatic discharge. I created the safety report for my leadership and briefed the rest of the deployed members on the events of the evening with a warning of similar situations they may encounter.

I was slated the next day to fly a similar mission in the same aircraft. After initial inspection, maintenance assured us the plane was OK and that it was no worse for wear. We heard and felt the same indications as the night prior following the initial engine run. For the first time in my short operational career with the 319th, I gave back to maintenance an aircraft that I claimed was broke before I even departed. Following further evaluation of the engine, maintenance found several bearings and parts welded together. They estimated the engine would've failed within the first hour if we had continued on a typical power setting for that mission. The engine was replaced within two weeks, and the plane was flying shortly thereafter. The amount of damage incurred by the event isn't typical of an electrostatic discharge, but then we can't rule out the possibility that we were actually struck by lightning. Either way, my luck bag is a little lighter, and my knowledge and experience bags are a little heavier.

NOTES:

CHAPTER 2
COMMUNICATION
CREW RESOURCE MANAGEMENT (C.R.M.)

"**We have two ears and one mouth so that we can listen twice as much as we speak.**"

Epictetus, Greek philosopher 55-135 AD

DECEPTIVE COMMUNICATIONS
C-130H, 39TH AIRLIFT SQUADRON, DYESS AFB, TEXAS

Captain Phillip Varilek, August 2008

This article addresses the principles of crew resource management and operational risk management in a combat environment. Although no recordable incident took place, the crew encountered multiple obstacles that hindered the success of an AirEvac mission and threatened the lives of the crew and medical staff onboard. Had CRM and ORM been sacrificed, prevailing obstacles would've led to mission failure and possibly the death of a wounded soldier relying on transport to a medical facility.

The 746th Expeditionary Airlift Squadron was a squadron of C-130Hs chopped to CENTCOM from Dyess Air Force Base, Texas. One responsibility of the squadron was to posture an aircraft and aircrew as an "A" Standby Force, with the capability of launching within one hour. One day in August, an aircraft launched on an emergency med evac mission to Tarin Kowt, an unsecured field in austere Afghanistan.

The aircrew typically had a low ORM score with a new aircraft commander being the limiting factor. Despite occasional stumbles in

CRM early in the deployment, the crew recently reached an efficient operating level and was focused on executing the critical mission. Though the ALFA Standby Force was alerted 14 hours into the "eligible for alert" window, any presence of complacency was overshadowed by enthusiasm.

Upon arrival at the aircraft, Tactics and Intel briefed the crew, while the medical crew director presided over the reconfiguration of the cargo compartment. With a systematic routine, complimented by efficient CRM, the aircraft was ready to taxi well within time constraints. However, the benefits enabled by proficient ground ops were negated by a cargo ramp malfunction, resulting in a delayed takeoff. Though this maintenance setback was frustrating, hindsight would show it as a minute impact to the overall mission.

Once airborne, we had a 4.5-hour transit, providing the aircrew with time to discuss their tactical approach. Although occupied by Coalition Forces, a secure perimeter wasn't established around the landing zone. Intel also briefed possible hostile activity within the area. "Blacked-out" ops, aided by night visions goggles, would be used on the approach to the infrared lit dirt landing zone. Unfortunately, Tarin Kowt is surrounded by heavy terrain, and there was negligible moon illumination and minimal cultural lighting to aid in field acquisition. The navigator would prove to be an invaluable resource as the only crew member aboard familiar with the field and its surrounding environment.

However, before descent into these unforgiving conditions, we had to establish communications with Tarin Kowt.

Typically, coordinating clearances into an airfield doesn't pose significant risks to an experienced aircrew. However, attempting to establish communications with a closed facility an hour earlier than expected can result in an undesirable situation. After continuous efforts on multiple frequencies, we entered a hold at an altitude driven by terrain and threat considerations. Despite tensions generated by the absence of two-way communications, the first transmission we received troubled the crew even more than the initial radio silence. A suspicious voice replied with an unfamiliar callsign and a thick Arabic accent. The suspect authority also issued the following nonstandard clearance: "You are cleared for whatever you want." Obviously, instruction wouldn't be accepted from a source that couldn't be authenticated. After assuming this encounter was a feeble attempt of deception by insurgents and being unable to contact a legitimate agency, the crew decided to divert to Bagram Air Base due to fuel considerations. While exiting the last orbit, an acknowledgement was finally received by an English controller at Tarin Kowt. The touchdown zone of the airfield was identified with extreme difficulty, despite using NVGs.

Shortly after leaving the security of high altitudes and committing to a tactical penetration descent, the crew observed a spotlight sweeping the black skies. Already within lethal range of surface-to-air missiles, there was limited maneuvering airspace to mitigate this threat due to the surrounding hazardous terrain. We had not visually acquired the IR LZ lights despite having positive position assurance from the GPS. After avoiding the search light, the crew was able to precisely navigate via the aircraft self-contained navigation system in tandem with a GPS-moving map display, but a low approach was required to acquire the LZ visually. The touchdown zone of the airfield was identified with extreme difficulty, despite the use of NVGs.

While attempting to keep the references in sight for a return low-altitude tactical approach, the crew was suddenly distracted by small-arms fire on the airfield boundary. Although not aimed at our aircraft, a precision maximum effort landing was imperative to deny the enemy another opportunity. Intensity in the cockpit thickened due to the several threats already encountered, the extreme concentration required to execute an assault landing on NVGs to a dirt runway, and the lack of outside lighting.

While using efficient CRM and within safe approach parameters, the landing was made without incident. They unloaded the patient under the cover of darkness, without shutting down the engines and through coordinated efforts between aircrew and ground support. After minimum turn time on the ground, a reverse departure was executed to deny the previously encountered small-arms fire.

Climb out to altitude and the final 45-minute leg was uneventful. Again, slight resistance was encountered upon arrival at Bagram Air Base due to the saturated maximum-on-ground capacity. Initially, we were instructed to hold by Bagram Approach. However, after placing justified emphasis on our callsign, an amended clearance was received, and the aircrew was given priority to land. Once on the deck, the critically wounded soldier was released to Bagram medical personnel.

Lessons Learned:

This "there I was" experience doesn't address a specific aircraft mishap, but demonstrates the application of CRM and ORM as observed personally by the co-pilot on the evacuation mission. The aircrew applied expertise originating with Intel and Tactics before departure, concluding with competence with aircrew and AE personnel upon arrival at Tarin Kowt. A reversion to micromanaging or any other breakdown in CRM wouldn't have allowed us to survive the complexity of the mission or the numerous threats encountered. And despite limited preparation time to accurately assess each hazard, the significance of the mission quantified the heightened risk. As demonstrated by the success of the mission, these principles were used in the prevention of a mishap versus their traditional role as a tool in investigating a mishap.

NOTES:

CALL ME ON IT!

HC-130, 58TH OPERATIONS SUPPORT SQUADRON, KIRTLAND AFB, N.M.

Major Ryan S. Kennedy, Winter 2012

"I didn't think we had done the checklist, but I didn't want to say anything."

It was a typical day sortie in the HC-130. We had done a low level, passed some fuel and provided training for the local HH-60s, accomplished airdrops, and then flew the pilot proficiency portion of the sortie. I was the instructor pilot tasked with completing the unit indoctrination for a newly-arrived instructor pilot (IP). I had been at the squadron only about four months myself and was just becoming comfortable with the local flying conditions. Except for the student loadmaster who had just spoken up, all the other crew members were mission-qualified instructors.

The flight was uneventful up to the point of getting instrument approaches for the IP undergoing indoc, as required by the syllabus. We'd worked with the approach controller to get as many different approaches into the field as possible. It was busy in the afternoon and meant we were vectored for what seemed like forever and then told to keep the speed up and configure late. The two hours of instrument work had apparently been enough to throw the crew out of our normal rhythms for checklist accomplishment. Our final approach to the full-stop landing was the last of quite a few, only this time neither of us piloting the aircraft remembered to check that the Before Landing Checklist had been called complete, and unfortunately the flight engineer missed the call, too. Luck was with us that day and, unlike several Air Force crews before and since, we had actually accomplished all the steps. That alone is what prevented a learning experience from becoming a mishap.

Once on the ground, the flight engineer realized he had never called the checklist complete. It was when we were in the debrief that the student loadmaster made his surprise statement, and I realized there had been at least one person on the airplane who could've prevented the entire discussion. The reason he hadn't spoken up is in the basics of crew resource management (CRM) taught in every refresher. As the junior member of the crew, he thought the instructors obviously knew more than he and he was afraid to speak up. In short, he had given us all halos.

Lessons Learned:

Although no damage or injury occurred that day, I have often used this example as a teaching tool for CRM and the whole-crew concept.

It's up to instructors and higher-time mission crew members to ensure that the young aviator has been empowered to speak up if there's something out of the ordinary. Many of us assume that since that's what's taught in the standard CRM courses, those young aviators are empowered. My experience that day taught me that's not true.

Whether on a crew airplane with a young enlisted troop or in a formation of fighters with a brand new wingman, it's the responsibility of those who've been flying for a while to point to the young guys and tell them face-to-face, "If it's dumb, dangerous or different, you call me on it." If our response is that we meant to do what we were doing, it's our further responsibility to explain ourselves fully in debrief so we don't inadvertently prevent that crew member from speaking up in another time or place and preventing a real mishap. I'm just glad that the day that student loadmaster decided not to say something my gear was actually down, and I pray that next time I screw up there's someone willing to step out and call me on it.

NOTES:

COMMUNICATION IN C.R.M.

B-52, 47TH FLYING TRAINING WING, LAUGHLIN AFB, TEXAS

Captain Darrick Mosely, Oct 2008

In the B-52, crew resource management is easy to appreciate. It shows up in every sortie and very often is in direct correlation to mission success.

On paper it's simple enough: the five-person crew works together under the leadership of the aircraft commander to navigate to the combat zone and put bombs on target while evading threats. A junior crew might see good CRM as a navigator telling the pilots that they are so many knots off airspeed while flying in the pattern. Strong CRM might also be the EW and the radar navigator learning how to coordinate their calls so they aren't talking over each other during a bomb run. These lessons are learned early on as crews hone their combat skills on regular training missions. I was no different.

I was concerned with putting the bombs on target and getting home. Then, under special circumstances, I learned to expand my CRM concept beyond the cockpit. I learned new CRM tricks, like using ATC's radar to tell just how dense that cloud formation is up ahead — nice to know before you take a jet limited to 2 Gs through a cloud bank without weather radar. These are great uses of CRM and they all have something important in common — they all rely on strong communication skills. In my everlasting quest to become a better pilot, I've learned that communication skills are integral to strong CRM.

Just when I thought I had a pretty good grasp on the subject, I made a crucial CRM mistake. It was while air refueling on a combat mission during Operation Enduring Freedom. We were in pre-contact over the Indian Ocean late on a pitch black night. As co-pilot, all I really had to do was monitor the boom through the hatch window and call out the relative distance from the receptacle as it went over my head. When we started into the contact position, I noticed that this particular boom operator was using the technique of pointing the boom at the co-pilot's windshield until the last possible second and then swinging it around for the plug in, which I'm not a big fan of. This particular boom operator lost that game of chicken that night when he didn't move the boom at the optimal time, and he scraped the boom along the top side of the aircraft in what appeared to be an attempt to pry my ejection hatch off the plane. This caught my attention. The shower of sparks that you can only get as you grind metal against metal caused me to express my displeasure with a number of expletives, but I offered no explanation of what I was seeing until my crew asked me. CRM lesson learned. With three crew dogs along for the ride who don't have windows to see how your AR is progressing, it's best not to say anything that gives them the impression that they're seconds away from burning up in a fiery mess, unless that's actually the case. They expressed their discontent with me, and rightly so. More than a simple communications issue, I denied the crew my perspective. My comments were reactionary, but I've found that a lot of flying is training yourself to react in the best way possible. Case in point:

Several months later in the early days of OIF, I found myself in another learning situation. My crew and I were attacking targets in the vicinity of Baghdad. It was another night sortie and I was in a formation with other bombers. I had seen the occasional pot shot taken at me before, but this night, I would see some intense resistance. As one SAM after another launched up from the ground (this time I was on the NVGs), I calmly called out each missile and the appropriate direction to evade. I sensed some frustration from my EW who commented that he wasn't picking up any signals. Once again, the crew found themselves along for the ride with little to do. We maneuvered aggressively on our way to the target and put the bombs on target as planned. Later, my crew told me they appreciated the calm manner in which I called out the enemy fire. It allowed them to remain calm and keep up their situational awareness, making us a more effective crew. While it's always nice to get praise, there was an important lesson that wasn't lost on me. Up until then, I didn't appreciate how uncomfortable and distracting it must be to know there are missiles in the air intended for you. Not only can't you do anything about it, but you must rely on someone else to tell you where they are. It goes to show that sometimes CRM isn't just using all of the assets at your disposal, but also being an asset for someone else.

My time as a buff co-pilot is over. Now I'm a T-38 IP trying to teach CRM to SUPT students. Some people see CRM at odds with the single-seat pilot mentality, but I think it's just the opposite. Without a crew to back you up, it's very important that you be aware of and take advantage of all your potential resources to effect a successful mission. I'm still learning great CRM lessons. Wingmen, ATC, cockpit instruments and prior preparation all play important roles in crew resource management, but a good set of communication skills work wonders. These days I challenge myself to use the most effective communication I can. If brevity really is the soul of wit, then sometimes silence must be genius. I find that almost as often as not, it's better for all involved to just take the jet and demonstrate what I'm talking about than talking my students through my CRM analysis process.

Lessons Learned:

I still can't say that I've mastered the concept of CRM, but I do know that I can make continual progress by working to improve my communication skills.

NOTES:

EGO VERSUS THE E-WORD
F-16, 354 FW/SEF, EIELSON AFB, AK

Major Jeremy "Smuggler" Jenness, May 2008

There is always a bit of rivalry between fighter pilots. As an F-15C driver, I would joke and laugh with my Eagle buddies when we heard of yet another of "those F-16 guys" who had to declare emergency fuel and gum up the return to base flow following a large force exercise at Nellis Air Force Base, Nev. With twice as many engines and more than twice as much fuel, there were times in the Eagle when I was low on gas, but never so low that I had to throw out the "E-word." It was a matter of pride, and yes, ego, that I always made it home without calling attention to myself. That is, until one night at Nellis, flying F-16s with the Aggressors, I became one of "those F-16 guys."

I was fairly new in the Fighting Falcon with less than 100 hours, and less than six of those at night. I had never flown at night at Nellis, and I had never fought from the west side of the Northern Ranges — the typical "bad guy" land. I had the only clean jet in our formation (no external fuel tanks) and was not fragged to go to the tanker to get more fuel. My job was to stay in the airspace for as long as I could to provide training and then RTB once I hit bingo fuel. Of course, as anyone will tell you who has flown fighters during Red Flag or a Weapons School LFE, even a simple RTB can be a chore, especially at night in a jet that doesn't have much fuel at engine start.

I hit bingo and removed from the fight to the west. I descended to FL190, exited the airspace over Stonewall, and prepared for the long trek home around the range complex. Having not done the recovery to Nellis from this direction, I immediately set max range airspeed and requested the most direct route I could from ATC. It wasn't long before ATC had some changes for me. In fact, three times they vectored me away from the standard recovery route for other aircraft exiting the airspace: first 30 degrees, then 20 more, then another 30. By that point, I wasn't even headed toward Nellis anymore, and the F-16 min fuel and emergency fuel numbers, as well as the techniques and options to resolve this situation, took a front seat in my mind.

The bingo fuel I used was appropriate to get back to Nellis with "normal recovery fuel." However, rarely is there a "normal recovery" during a night LFE at Nellis, and I needed to think of some non-normal options. One option was to land at Creech Air Force Base, which I would practically fly right over during the RTB. During the day, in VFR conditions, this was perfectly reasonable. However, with no viable precision approach into Creech, this wasn't really feasible for a dark Nevada night. Another option was to cancel my IFR clearance, cut in front of "the train" returning from the ranges, and do a visual straight in back at Nellis. Due to my lack of experience with this recovery, coupled with my lack of night experience in the F-16 and at Nellis, I ruled out this option before even stepping that night — it was a matter of my personal operational risk management. Another option was to ask for priority in the recovery pattern. At that moment, I calculated I would be below my normal recovery fuel, but still above min fuel. I was also vectored back on course as ATC finally fit me into "the train."

My recovery was back on track, but I maintained a very heightened sense of my fuel state and approach control vectors to aircraft in front of me. Everyone seemed to be getting a normal instrument downwind and turn to base. Those normal vectors stopped with the two-ship of F-16s that was in front of me. There was a dramatic pause from approach control as we both continued on downwind, flowing north, farther from Nellis. The calculator in my brain now had to recalculate what fuel state I would now recover with. The two-ship in front spoke up as I was running my numbers and slowing to my max endurance airspeed. They were given what seemed like a base turn, but was actually a box pattern across the final approach course.

Then it was my turn to start that slow process of shoving my ego to the side. "Approach, Sniper 2, min fuel, looking for a base turn." "Sniper 2, Nellis Approach, copy." Well, I'd taken that first step, but I was still flying away from Nellis. After what seemed like an eternity, approach finally came back with, "Sniper 2, approach, we informed tower, but it didn't work, continue heading 360." Great. In a single-engine multi-role fighter without much gas, the margin between minimum fuel and emergency fuel isn't that great. It took a couple more calls to approach to figure out that the tower was trying to launch a couple flights of F-18s on opposite direction takeoffs. While I had a small margin of gas, the expected delay was at least 10 minutes. With the DME to Nellis growing larger by the second, that margin had become negligible. The pressure was building, and I gave my ego another shove.

> "Approach, Sniper 2, if you're going to delay me that much, then I will definitely be emer-fuel," I stated matter-of-factly, and though I had taken two large steps in that direction, I was still two syllables short of throwing out the "E-word."

After a moment, Approach asked if I had the two-ship of F-16s still in sight and if I could follow them. I could see the lights of their formation, so I turned right on what I considered a base leg. As I flew toward them and picked up a radar lock, it became obvious to me that they were in a right turn in their box pattern. I would end up meeting them 180 degrees out. I had no intention of adding a night intercept to this situation, so again I had to do some more coordinating with Approach control. Between me, the other two-ship, and everything else Approach was handling, I could tell he was getting a bit task-saturated. So finally, with one last kick, my ego went tumbling into the Nevada desert.

> "Approach, Sniper 2 is Emergency Fuel, Nellis in sight, proceeding on a visual straight in for Runway 21L."

Finally. Despite my efforts to keep a low profile, I made it known I was an F-16, low on gas, and needed priority to land. It had a huge effect. Approach control seemed almost relieved, radio transmissions returned to a normal level, and final approach, the weight and pressure, which may have well been my ego, was lifted. I was definitely emergency fuel, but my seat cushion returned to its normal position, and I knew I was home free. All it took was to be "that guy" and make that last radio call, and I was glad I did.

Lessons Learned:

The lessons are fairly obvious, even to a young wingman. I had certainly learned those lessons before, but sometimes even experienced pilots need a refresher course. If you're unsure and unfamiliar with the mission or procedures, add some extra gas for your own bingo and comfort level, especially at night. Regardless of whether some people consider emergency fuel an actual emergency or just poor planning, if you need to, then declare it to get your aircraft and your body back on the ground — that's why it's called "emergency" fuel. As for me, next time I plan to cut southwest, exit the ranges much closer to Nellis, and take that visual straight in. It was what I ended up doing, anyway. Besides, that evening significantly lowered my ORM assessment of doing that straight-in at night.

As I made one of my best landings, night or day, F-15 or F-16, that evening, I had to chuckle to myself. The radio was alive again with the two-ship of F-16s, now behind me, negotiating with tower.

> "Negative, we're landing behind Sniper 2. We're not ready to call the E-word yet, but we're getting close on gas."

NOTES:

CHAPTER 3
FATIGUE

"The experienced fighting pilot does not take unnecessary risks. His business is to shoot down enemy planes, not to get shot down."

Captain Eddie Rickenbacker, USAS

FLYING WHILE FATIGUED
KC-135, 18 OSS/OSOST, KADENA AB, JAPAN

Captain Ryan Truschinski, April 2008

Fatigue is a factor we all deal with. From loss of sleep to crossing multiple time zones, we run into different facets of fatigue. Many factors contribute to fatigue, and each is just as bad as the others. We have several fail-safes in place to help fight off fatigue, the main one being getting adequate sleep. The Air Force mandates that a flying crew has 12 hours of crew rest with eight uninterrupted hours for sleep. This is a good rule, seeing as eight hours is the recommended amount of sleep. However, in order for these fail-safes to be effective, they need to be used. Fatigue has a way of catching up with you when you least want it to. Just like when you're driving, fatigue can creep up on you. However, unlike driving, in the air, you don't have much of a choice as to when you can pull over and get some rest.

Early in 2003 during the start of OIF, flying operations were on a continuous basis. I was a crew member on a KC-135 deployed in the AOR for the beginning of the air campaign. We found ourselves flying continually and getting the minimum crew rest before going on another mission. This minimum crew rest met the requirements for getting the recommended time for sleep, but because of the duration of the mission, we found that our show times would slowly slip further into the day, so that within a week, we would be on the opposite time of day. So, on one Sunday we would show at 8 a.m., and by the next Sunday, our show time would be 8 p.m. This did nothing to help get our circadian rhythm settled down. When you checked on an individual, day-to-day rest was adequate, but looking at the trends over several days would show that the situation was not ideal.

On a routine flight, we would have one or two crew members taking short naps, either on the way out to the AR or on the way back to base. Sometimes they'd nap on both legs. The main reason was that, for the most part, we would have almost three hours of cruise time to get to and from our AR track. About half of the cruise time would be in areas where there wasn't radio contact with any controllers or receivers. The one thing I can equate this to would be driving through the Iowa countryside. You get a hypnotic constancy where nothing changes, and you slowly phase out with the lack of outside stimuli. Not only that, but out in the AOR, there are areas of very little light, especially at night. Before you know it, sleep may rear its ugly head.

The crews I was flying with each had two or more deployments under their belts. I was on my fourth deployment. All of us were current and qualified and had seen the same missions multiple times before. I hate to say it, but I'm sure there was some level of complacency in our approach to the mission, and I'm sure our crew was not the only one.

With the constant slip in our flying window, I was not sleeping as soundly as I usually do. On top of that, I was dealing with jet lag, uncomfortable cots, and the occasional construction project in the middle of tent city. Instead of sleeping for the eight hours provided, I found myself going to the chow hall for the different meal times, because of the lack of consistency in rest times. The basic thought I had was that it was better to get food than to toss and turn without getting sleep. I was experiencing some sleep deprivation by the time our crew show time came around, and we walked over to ops as the sun was setting. We sat through the regular briefings from Intel, Weather and Ops. The mission was fairly routine, with no weather affecting our route. After our crew brief, we grabbed our gear and headed out to the jet. The drive lasted about 10 minutes, and I'm pretty sure I napped for about eight of those minutes. Being tired enough to nap was a clear indicator that fatigue had a hold of me already.

Once we got to the jet, the preflight through takeoff was uneventful, and we proceeded with the mission. On the way out, the boom operator took a nap, so he'd be fresh for the refueling. The rest of the crew played a name game to pass the time. One person would give a name of a movie character, and the next person had to use the first letter of the last name, and use it as the first letter in a first name. For example, James Bond could be the first name, and Barney Rubble would be a valid following name. Anyway, we got to 30 minutes from refueling and configured everything for the rendezvous. Refueling went as planned, and once the receiver was off and clear, we started heading back to base. We checked off with our controlling agency and entered the portion of the route where we had a break in radio coverage. On top of that, there was very little light in the sky and on the ground, so it was almost basically complete darkness outside the jet.

With no radio coverage and very little to see outside the windows, the crew began feeling tired. The boom operator fell asleep in his seat, which really didn't bother the rest of the crew, as there was nothing going on. The co-pilot decided he would also take a quick nap until we got back into radio coverage. The aircraft commander was OK with this, and said he would be able to monitor the jet, while I backed him up. We were good to go with two crew members watching the jet, while the other two got some rest. As time went along, I slowly found myself getting very tired, with the occasional head-bob. After each, I'd quickly check on the pilot and where we were, just to make sure everything was still good to go. One head-bob turned into an unplanned 15- to 20-minute power nap. That, in itself, would not have been that bad, as long as the pilot was keeping track of things.

As I slowly woke out of my nice little nap, my eyes adjusted to the darkness in the cockpit, and I looked around to see what was going on. Next to me, I found the boom operator fast asleep in his seat, exactly where I last remembered him. I next looked up to the pilot seats and checked on the co-pilot. He also was fast asleep. I checked the time, and found that I had been out for at least 15 minutes. I then looked at our position, and found we had another 15 minutes before we got back into radio contact. I looked back up to talk to the pilot and let him know about my falling asleep, and to check to see if I had missed anything. That's when I finally noticed that the pilot was also fast asleep! I reached over and shook his shoulder and woke him up. He quickly came to, and his eyes suddenly got really wide, probably as wide as mine. We suddenly realized that the autopilot had been the only thing keeping us flying for anywhere up to 15 minutes, while all four of us were oblivious to the world.

We debriefed this and implemented different techniques to ensure that never happened again. One of these was not allowing more than one person to sleep at a time. We were very lucky that nothing happened while we were asleep, and I'm positive that the unique situation we were in helped us, and that it never went beyond just a learning experience. We could easily have had a mishap if anything had gone wrong, with no one able to react to it. Many factors built up the level of fatigue we all had, and it was not readily apparent to us at first. Crews need to be aware of these things and need to take their crew rest very seriously. As a last resort, if the crew is too tired to fly the mission, they should consider not flying until they get the rest they need.

Lessons Learned:

Luck can only carry you so far — everything else falls on you being ready and able.

Get some rest.

<u>NOTES:</u>

BREAKING THE ERROR CHAIN
C-17, OPERATIONAL INFORMATION WITHHELD

Name withheld by request, Spring 2012

Fatigue is inevitable in the aviation community. Every crew member can probably cite at least one example. We don't perform at our best when we're tired. We try to mitigate fatigue but know flying isn't a good idea when all mitigation measures fail. So what happens when someone says you're not allowed to call "safety of flight"?

There I was – an aircraft commander for six months and starting to gain some confidence. At four weeks into Operation Iraqi Freedom, my hard-working crew had flown two weeks without downtime. We flew, landed and were back at it 12 hours later.

On one particular day, I could tell we were dragging from the start, and we talked about our fatigue level. Everyone said they'd crashed during the 12 hours of crew rest, taking only enough time to eat and shower. We took off uneventfully and flew a combat mission. As we headed back, we started the checklist and were soon on the ground. But wait. Did we finish the checklist? Did we get clearance to land? What just happened?

We evidently finished the checklist because all the switches were in the right position, and the tower verified that we had clearance to land. However, none of us could remember, although the process occurred just five to 10 minutes earlier. I knew then that we'd been lucky, but we were headed down a bad road. We discussed it later and concluded that we were probably micro sleeping on final.

Despite our best efforts to be responsible and get sleep, we needed to do something more. We collectively decided that 16 hours off, instead of the normal 12, would be enough. After all, we were at war. A day off would be unreasonable.

I went to the ops desk, described our activities over the last week and what happened the day before and requested 16 hours. When he said no, I explained again, in more detail, why we needed four more hours. I was flabbergasted when, again, the answer was, "No." I told him that if we got alerted in 12 hours – and we were as tired as we were that day – I would call "safety of flight." He responded, "That's not allowed." I then asked to see someone in his chain of command and was told to stand by as he went behind closed doors. Sometime later, he returned and said we would be legal in 16 hours. It wasn't easy, but we had successfully broken the error chain and probably prevented a mishap.

Several years later, a crew in my squadron ran into a similar situation. That crew was alerted at home station in the late afternoon as an augmented crew for what was supposed to be a quick flight to pick up cargo then a longer flight across the ocean. At crew show, the crew members said they had tried to sleep in but had difficulty, which is fairly normal for a late evening alert. They thought they could figure out a good work rest plan to continue the mission as planned and were confident they'd all get enough sleep.

As the day progressed, they ran into several maintenance issues. The problems kept arising until they'd pounded the ramp long enough to reassess their fatigue levels and realized they were in the severe range. They called the controlling agency and were told that putting the crew to bed was best. The crew had no idea what was about to transpire.

What seemed to be the right crew decision to stop short of its intended destination due to fatigue turned into a bigger issue. Upon completion of that mission, the crew members were questioned about their "irresponsible" behavior. The entire squadron was briefed on that crew's decision, and leadership presented it as an example of what not to do.

The crew felt on that particular day, and in that set of circumstances, they made the right call. They likely broke the error chain.

As a senior ranking member in my squadron, I voiced my concerns to leadership about their approach. I remembered what it was like as a young aircraft commander to tell someone that the crew was fatigued and being told there would be no change. I wasn't successful in communicating this to leadership. Leadership sometimes doesn't see the situation the same way that the person making the decision sees it.

I present these two situations for a couple of reasons. First, if you are the young aircraft commander out there, make the right decision. Don't be afraid to say that you're too fatigued and unsafe to proceed. Second, as a leader, it's important to listen to your crews. Are they really irresponsible? Is their decision really a bad one?

Lessons Learned:

Every crew has a different dynamic and sometimes the error chain is broken. Sometimes, it isn't. A crew who breaks the chain is never wrong in breaking the chain. There may be lessons learned, but they are alive to learn them.

NOTES:

CHAPTER 4
UNEXPECTED EVENTS

"The flight was going fine until all of a sudden there was a boom. Dave looked at me and, 'We're in trouble'."

Lieutenant Colonel Dick Rutan, USAF

THE RACCOON AND THE ROCKET
TITAN ROCKET, HEADQUARTERS AIR FORCE SPACE COMMAND, PETERSON AFB, COLO.

Joseph Fury, Winter 2012

We put a lot of effort into making space launch operations safer by identifying hazards and eliminating, controlling or managing them. Some mishaps occur when there's an event or chain of events that we haven't previously considered. The following series of events actually happened and almost impacted our assured access to space.

Background

The Titan rocket used two large strap-on solid rocket motors that weighed 542,700 pounds apiece, and each generated 1.4 million pounds of thrust. These nine-story tall motors arrived at the launch base in cylindrical segments that were 10 feet tall and 10 feet in diameter. They were inspected and stored in the Receipt, Inspection and Storage (RIS) Building. These segments were assembled into the nine-story tall motors. The RIS Building could contain up to 1 million pounds of solid rocket propellant. Of course, smoking in or near the building was prohibited. In fact, spark or fire-producing devices, such as matches or cigarette lighters, were not allowed in the building. There was a guardhouse at the entrance to the enclosed RIS area. A raccoon had frequented that area for two weeks. One quiet evening at about 10 p.m., the departing guard told his replacement that they had a "tug of war" with the raccoon.

Sequence of Events

At 10:20 p.m., the guard was bitten by the raccoon and the chain of events began. At 10:30 p.m., other guards responded to allow the bitten guard to go to the hospital. The responding guards chased the raccoon into the RIS Building administrative area. Base entomology (animal control) was called to catch the raccoon so that it could be tested for rabies to determine if the bitten guard needed rabies shots. A trap was set in a hallway at 3:50 a.m., but by 7 a.m. the raccoon hadn't taken the bait. The entomologists noticed broken ceiling tiles and assumed the raccoon was hiding in the false ceiling. The bitten guard's doctor sent word that the capture of the raccoon should be given a high priority. The entomologists decided to set off a smoke bomb to drive the raccoon out of hiding. The building manager was called and he told the entomologists of the extreme fire danger and recommended that the fire department be consulted. The fire department misunderstood the building number and said that the smoke bomb would be OK, but they dispatched a fire truck to standby. Security police provided the smoke bombs. Two smoke bombs were placed in a metal trash can, ignited and placed in the overhead ceiling. The smoke bombs shot out a 2-foot flame and immediately caused the overhead insulation to burst into flames in a building containing approximately 1 million pounds of solid rocket propellant. The fire truck crew put out the building flames and the smoke bombs. The raccoon hadn't been caught, so the bitten guard received the rabies shots. What started as a small puncture wound from a raccoon almost ended in the destruction of a set of flight hardware and a facility needed to launch critical space systems. The loss could have cost the Air Force roughly $30 million, plus the delay in launching on-orbit capabilities.

Lessons Learned:

This chain of events began after duty hours and continued through the early-morning hours of the next day. The ensuing raccoon chase caused people to lose focus on their primary responsibilities for resource protection and safety. Proper reporting and approval procedures weren't followed. Entomology failed to follow proper procedures in obtaining the smoke bombs; the fire department failed to follow proper procedures for review and approval of the use of potentially explosive devices; there were delays in notifying appropriate building contractor personnel and the owning Air Force organization's management and facility custodians weren't well trained on their responsibilities.

Are you and your team prepared to maintain focus on your responsibilities when unusual things happen?

A raccoon was later spotted walking in the rafters of the high bay of the RIS. A raccoon was eventually trapped two days later, but no one could positively identify the raccoon as the one that bit the guard, and it was freed.

NOTES:

CHAPTER 5
IN-FLIGHT EMERGENCY

"If you're faced with a forced landing, fly the thing as far into the crash as possible."

First Lieutenant Bob Hoover, USAF

MURPHY'S GUNSHIP

AC-130, OPERATIONAL INFORMATION WITHHELD

Name withheld by request, Nov 2008

It looked to be another boring conclusion to another dull mission until the co-pilot put the gear handle down on final approach. The old Chinese curse says, "May you live in interesting times." When our AC-130's left main gear continued to show that the gear was in transit instead of the usual, comforting down and locked, the lives of 14 crew members suddenly became interesting, and that was only the beginning.

We had to execute a go-around and entered the pattern to try again. The pilots cycled the gear with the same result: left side stuck in transit. The loadmaster took a look through a small portal over the wheel well and visually confirmed that the gear was out of position. He could see that something, possibly a rag, was jammed in there and preventing the gear from coming down all the way. Try as he might, he couldn't dislodge the object. We weren't going to get the gear all the way down and locked. In that position, it would crumple under the aircraft weight and leave us sliding down the runway on our belly, spewing sparks and possibly departing said runway in God knows what direction. Maybe into some parked fires or a fuel pit? And since we were a gunship returning from an uneventful mission, we could also contribute a full combat load of 105 mm and 40 mm ammunition to the proceedings.

After notifying tower of our predicament and with their clearance, we climbed back up to altitude to work the problem. The aircraft commander and navigator agreed that it would be best to hold over the nearby range where we normally test-fire and tweak our guns. As fire-control officer, I gave the pilots computer guidance for an orbit over our usual target area. We were well clear of airfield traffic, and the pilots had something easy to fly while working the gear issue.

Once established in our orbit, the flight engineer went to the back and confirmed the LM's assessment. He consulted the flight manuals and concluded that the only course of action was to use the emergency tie-down straps. Once in place, our hope was that these straps would keep the gear in place during the stress of landing. Sounded simple enough. This procedure is rarely practiced and requires considerable dexterity and patience to properly execute. The FE, LM, and aerial gunners would all be involved in the effort, but even the most experienced among them confessed to only practicing it once in training. They further recalled that it was quite the challenge even at 0 mph in a classroom setting. Fortunately, the flight manual in this instance was clearly written and included helpful diagrams. With one gunner reading and another dispensing straps, the others set about the delicate task.

It was a slow, grueling process. The space available for them to work was far from ample, lighting was poor, and the slipstream made proper placement of the straps a labor of Hercules. Meanwhile, we were holding at length over the same point on the ground — never a tactically sound thing to do, and now even less so since the sun was coming up. We were now plainly visible in the morning light, so the electronic warfare officer opted to start punching off pre-emptive flares. There was no danger of highlighting our position, as there was no more question of hiding in darkness anyway. IR-trackers would now have difficulty tracking us, and we were steadily lightening the load of flares we'd have onboard for a possible belly landing. The remainder would be jettisoned on final approach over a safe patch of ground.

Fuel was becoming a concern, but for now we had enough since we were minutes from the base. Finally, the crew in the back announced their triumphant placement of the tie-down straps on the afflicted gear. It had been dicey, with the limited number of straps nearly being lost in the slipstream.

After some crew discussion, the AC decided to get clearance to go hot on the firing range to try to shoot out all our ammo. Jettisoning all of it would be very time-consuming and would create a less-safe condition on the ground. As FCO, I opted for dual-target attack mode, which uses both guns simultaneously, to expeditiously expend all our rounds. We executed the pre-strike checklist, the sensor operators visually cleared the impact area, and we were ready to go. I ran through my final procedure and gave the guns to the pilot. He and the sensor operators pressed their triggers and ... nothing.

Our second problem of the night: fire-control issues. In this case, the hydraulic-trainable gun mounts were not driving the guns to the correct angles for firing at our current flight regime. The mission computer recognized the aiming discrepancy and refused to pass a firing pulse to the guns. I began my normal troubleshooting, but time was critical — the sun was rising and gas was burning. The AC wisely suggested I switch to a degraded fire mode, which bypassed the computer's safety inhibits. I did so and the firing commenced, though with only one gun at a time. As suspected, the rounds landed way off, since the guns were pointed incorrectly. There was no quick fix to this in the air. The guns' inaccuracy was an annoyance, but not critical. The rounds were still striking well inside the range area with plenty of room to spare, and the misses were consistent, not wandering off. Most importantly, we were lightening our net explosive weight for our uncertain landing. Back at the base, there was a missing man ceremony. Onlookers thought it was impressive that a gunship turned out for a daylight shoot, complete with flare launchings, for the commemoration.

Meanwhile, our condition got further complicated when the No. 4, right outboard, engine's prop low oil light came on for a bit and then extinguished during the shoot. The FE judged that oil was indeed getting low, but he was comfortable keeping the engine running for now. He recommended to the AC, who agreed, that they should shut that engine down on short final and feather the prop, lest it suddenly seize up on its own and remain unfeathered when we're low and slow. That would cause a wallop of drag on the right side at a critical time — an already complicated landing wherein we wanted to land on the left gear as late as possible, as it might not hold up.

By this time, the crew felt that it was in one of those ridiculously overloaded emergency procedure simulators. You know the ones where so much goes wrong at once that you think, "This would never actually happen." Wrong. Murphy wasn't quite done with us.

During the course of the firing, the hydraulics near the guns developed another problem: springing a geyser of a leak all over the now-heated 105 mm gun. As soon as the fluid hit the hot metal, we had severe smoke and fumes in the cargo compartment, so bad that it was IMC back there and getting smoky even on the flight deck.

We ceased fire immediately, donned oxygen masks and flipped them to 100 percent. It was at this point that we became concerned. Once everyone checked in on oxygen, the AC announced, "All right, @#*% this, we're going to land ASAP." No one argued. The plane didn't want to fly any more today. Fortunately, the hydraulics problem was confined to the utility system — we still had flight controls. We completed our post-strike checklist and shut down the guns. We still carried almost half our ammo load, but we could no longer shoot and hadn't the time to jettison. The lead gunner had the presence of mind to inspect the tie-down straps again, in case they jarred loose during the shooting. Verdict: good to go.

The co-pilot declared an emergency with tower and got us clearance for a long, straight-in approach. After running the checklists, they set us up on final. We removed the flight deck overhead escape hatch both to disperse the smoke and to provide a ready exit in case we needed it after landing. On short final, the EWO jettisoned the remaining flares, as planned. The pilots and FE shut down No. 4 engine and feathered the prop, so we'd get no nasty surprises from it while trying to land as delicately as possible. I thought it good that our pilots practice three-engine stuff all the time. The AC touched down first on the untroubled right gear, then, as gently as possible, let us down on the tied-down left gear. It held, and we taxied clear of the active runway. After shutdown, we egressed the aircraft, as we'd briefed, because of the persistent smoke and fumes. No casualties, and the plane would fly again within days.

Lessons Learned:

Because my duty position meant I was mostly not involved in the emergency, I was able to observe the crew response relatively unfettered. From the veteran AC down to the rookie LM, the crew exhibited excellent CRM principles. No one forgot the priorities of aviate, navigate and communicate while working the various problems. Information flowed readily between crew positions on the 14-member crew, and always at the proper time. Needed tasks were accomplished with the requisite sense of urgency, but not a hint of overly hurried panic. "Slow is smooth, smooth is fast," as they say.

The crew's effective combination of thoughtful analysis and methodical accomplishment at each stage, properly coupled with a due sense of urgency, demonstrated excellent CRM principles and led to a successful recovery.

NOTES:

SAY SOMETHING... ANYTHING

OPERATIONAL INFORMATION WITHHELD, 505TH
OPERATIONS GROUP, PATRICK AFB, FLA

Captain Tyler Wickham, Nov 2008

All in all, I'd say I'm a pretty lucky guy. Lucky in life. Lucky in love. And definitely lucky in the cockpit. All of us have had our fair share of experiences we wish we'd only have to do in the simulator. Engine shutdowns, smoke in the cockpit, gear not down and locked ... you get the point. But if I'm writing an article about them, it means I really have very little to complain about. What gets you through these problems, benign or complex in nature? Systems knowledge, good checklist discipline, sound judgment and airmanship are some of the big ones. Oh, and a little bit of luck can go a long way.

Instead of luck, call it "trusting your instincts." When something doesn't feel right, you speak up. You get that little voice in the back of your brain telling you, "Hey, say something — this shouldn't be happening." It's not luck, but rather a trust of what you know is right and what your body is telling you. Back to my co-piloting days, I learned a lesson one day, and it's a lesson I still use today, every time I fly.

It was a daytime pilot-proficiency sortie; take off from home base, hit a tanker for some air refuelling work, and roll back to base for some IFR and VFR pattern work. Talk about sweet — three or four pilots getting to fly around to their hearts' content! The sortie began as normal, with an overcast deck dropping into the picture at about 2,000 feet. I've personally always preferred that; it's great practice for instrument work, but still allows for a VFR pattern. Our takeoff and cruise to the tanker were about as smooth as they get. No issues to note and the training was great. It was when we returned to the pattern that things got a bit weird.

I was a co-pilot with minimal hours and still trying to find a "feel" for the jet. I could fly engine-out approaches, landings and touch-and-gos, but by no means were they perfect. I was in the right seat, with my instructor in the left. We were flying our first approach and had already simulated the loss of an engine. Checklists were run, outside agencies were notified, and my entire crew was on the same page. Three-engine touch to a four-engine go to a simulated engine failure, takeoff continued. The purpose of a SEFTOC is to practice flying the jet if you lose an engine just after your decision speed and need to continue the takeoff.

We got the jet configured and brought it in for a nice touch-and-go, all four spooling up and rotating off the ground just like we always do. However, when I was airborne again, I felt a violent rolling tendency that I wasn't expecting. Then, at 200 feet, there goes the IP taking my No. 1 throttle to idle. Wow, now this was bad. I could barely keep the jet level, let alone fly it where I wanted to. It was the combination of that violent roll, coupled with the yaw from the simulated engine-out, all compounded by having to push the other three engines up to compensate for the loss of my No. 1. This was more than weird; it was downright wrong. Scary wrong. I couldn't shake the feeling that I was causing the roll. It had been so long since I'd flown three-engine approaches that I thought it was me.

It was time to get cleaned up and turn back into the IFR pattern for another approach. Talk about a handful of airplane. I have an engine out, rudder in to compensate for that, and the powerful rolling tendency that I was correcting with more than 50 percent opposite yoke input. I was at max effort just getting my gear and flaps up. I barely had any control authority left for the turn. I was really feeling scared. My instructor looked at me, wondering why my turn was all of about 15 degrees, and saw my hands full. He began to ask what was going on, but by that point, I had enough. Quickly, I said, "Sir, something is just not right, and I don't think it's me. I'm putting No. 1 back in and I'm going to figure this out." As No. 1 spooled back in, that helped. It eased the yaw that I had been controlling with rudder. But I still had a very noticeable roll to the left. I was controlling it with right yoke control, but that was nuts. A clean, equal-throttle airplane doesn't need more than 50 percent right yoke to fly level. Maybe the flaps didn't retract properly, or an engine wasn't producing thrust like it should, but something was definitely wrong.

By then, the IP took the jet and quickly noticed the roll. Immediately, he made the same face I'd made about 60 seconds before. You know that face — the one that says, "Something's really wrong, and I'm not sure I can fix it." He took the jet and flew a four engine low approach to get a feel for the controllability. The next approach was the IP's full stop. I was just glad to be on the ground.

We didn't even need to get out of the jet before maintenance started grilling us with questions. Why did we land early? Why did we fly that low approach? What was wrong? Honestly, we could only guess. The IP, the engineer and I started to explain when I heard a voice pipe in. It was one of the maintenance guys. "Let me guess, it was rolling on you and you didn't know why." Yup, but how did he know? "Your left spoiler — one set is stuck up about six to eight inches." That would do it.

Why that spoiler wouldn't fall flush to the wing after working perfectly for the first two hours of flight is beyond me, but it didn't, making for one scary touch-and-go.

During debrief, we all talked about the incident and what we could have done better. My big mistake was waiting. What did I think I was going to do? I knew something was wrong, but I kept trying to fix it myself until I just couldn't handle it anymore. I physically couldn't make the airplane do what I wanted, and that was the first time I said anything. If that's your mindset, why have a crew airplane? What harm would have come from my saying something sooner? None. I'm thankful that nothing really came of it, but it could have been much worse.

As it turned out, there was a malfunction in the hydraulic valve leading to the set of spoilers that wasn't allowing all the fluid out, therefore, not allowing it to lie flush on the wing. A tiny bit of spoilers raised on the top of the wing can decrease your lift pretty significantly.

In the end, my crew was praised for great aircraft control and crew coordination, but it was more a learning experience for me than it was time to pat myself on the back.

Lessons Learned:

From that one experience, I learned that there's no reason to keep a secret to yourself, especially on a crew aircraft. Even if you're completely wrong and it's something you should have known — big deal! It's always better to speak up and say something, say anything, than to lead your airplane, your crew and yourself into a situation you can't get out of.

NOTES:

FLIGHT EMERGENCY
C-130 HERCULES, 40TH AIRLIFT SQUADRON, DYESS AFB, TEXAS

Captain Eric Barada, Winter 2012

Twenty minutes after takeoff, the hydraulic pressure dropped below normal and turned our mission into anything but routine. Of the C-130's three hydraulic systems, the utility is arguably the most important since it powers the flaps, half of the flight controls, landing gear, normal anti-skid brakes and nose wheel steering. Our hydraulic reservoir was empty.

    The pilot confirmed she had the controls while the co-pilot declared an emergency and got vectors back home. We covered initial procedures and analysed the emergency. The navigator got the Dash 1 manual out after confirming our heading and altitude. One loadmaster communicated to the passengers while the other removed armor to steward emergency egress. The engineer went back to the cargo compartment. We circled the field on night vision goggles. After accomplishing the emergency checklist, we covered every possibility we could think of while burning down fuel. We lowered the flaps early in the emergency to ensure a normal landing. The landing gear showed down and locked; however, there was no guarantee it wouldn't collapse. The nose wheel steering wouldn't function, which could cause us to depart the runway. Emergency actions for both of these were covered by each crew member.

At best, this would be a normal 50 percent flap landing. At worst, our gear would collapse, and the props would hit the ground. We notified tower of our intentions and accomplished normal checklists to land. The pilot set the airplane down softly to give the landing gear a fighting chance and rolled out to a stop on the runway. Everyone exhaled a sigh of relief. Maintenance found a leak between engine 1 and 2 – not something that could be found during routine inspections.

Although we had an uncommon problem, this was as close to a by-the-book as a C-130 emergency can get. How we used crew resource management is worth noting.

Lessons Learned:

Our crew had been deployed almost two months and had gelled into an experienced team. We knew we were approaching the time in the deployment when complacency is common for C-130 crews. We consciously fought this problem by applying discipline to pre-briefs and checklist items. Sometimes that took real work.

Communication and delegation were vital. When the navigator went heads down to read the Dash 1, he told the pilot exactly where we were headed and any obstacles in our flight path. The engineer did the same for the co-pilot to switch fuel tanks for fuel balancing. The loadmasters enlisted the help of passengers to remove armor covering the doors. The good communication and thoroughness were being constantly attacked by fatigue.

Other traits that helped us succeed were a deep knowledge of how the systems work and maintaining a respectful, honest crew. The aircraft commander set the tone. Crew members weren't hesitant to say what they thought, but it was tempered with respect. This came from taking the time to learn each other's job. This emergency could have been much more difficult. We could've been too low on fuel to talk through the possibilities, or the weather could've prevented easy navigation over the airfield. The leak could've occurred inside the airplane, creating a health problem for everyone on board. These are the scenarios we should consider when things go well in order to build knowledge for the next emergency.

NOTES:

SINGLE-SEAT CREW DUTIES

A-10, 25TH FIGHTER SQUADRON, OSAN AB, KOREA

Captain Brian Burgoon, Spring 2012

If you read any Dash 1 flight manual on how to fly a single-seat fighter, you'll inevitably come to Section IV, Crew Duties. Fighter pilots pride ourselves on independence and even joke about the contents of this section at roll calls. The usual banter starts when the "Mayor" calls for a reading from Dash 1. A young lieutenant turns to Section IV and reads "Crew Duties," followed by the crowd responding in unison, "Not applicable!"

The truth is, the formation you fly with acts as one big crew. When your crew is on the same page, you're able to complete tasks in a condensed period of time and without sacrificing safety.

Last spring, I experienced an engine fire shortly after takeoff. The fire was inextinguishable. The pilots I flew with in the four-ship formation of A-10s acted as a single, well-orchestrated symphony to assist me in recovering the aircraft.

I was No. 4 in a four-ship upgrade sortie just south of the Korean Demilitarized Zone. The weather was average for the Korean spring with four to five miles of haze and a mid-level broken-to-overcast layer. We took off from Osan AB and performed a boresight on our Maverick missiles. Upon reaching 5,500 feet altitude, I went heads down to perform my checks. I finished my checks 10 miles out from Osan, and that's when I got the first indication of a problem. I instantly lost rightsize hydraulic pressure and got a hydraulic reservoir warning light indicating the level of fluid was low.

I also had a bleed air leak light, indicating extremely hot air entering the fuselage and possible fire. I did what we all do when faced with an emergency and thought, "Oh crap, why me?" Then, my training kicked in, and I informed the rest of the formation of my aircraft malfunctions. We were 15 miles from Osan, and I requested to turn back and have No. 3 rejoin to the chase position. The flight lead cleared me off, and I started a 180-degree turn back to Osan.

As I began the turn, my right engine started to lose oil pressure. I asked No. 3 to move into chase position and look over my right engine because I was about to shut it down. As No. 3 moved into position, he informed me the right engine was on fire. At the same time I got that alarming call over the radio, I noticed my right fire handle was illuminated. I executed the bold face procedure to extinguish the engine fire and discharged one of the two A-10C fire bottles. Normally, that would extinguish the fire and the pilot would be able to recover the aircraft to the nearest suitable airfield on the remaining good engine. Unfortunately, the one fire bottle didn't extinguish the flames. No. 3 was flying a few hundred feet behind and said he saw the fire go out while the fire agent was spraying, but then the flames kicked up again. I then quickly used the second fire bottle. It had the same result. I was now out of extinguishing agent and had to focus on getting the plane on the deck before the fire spread to other parts of the aircraft.

All this took place within six to nine minutes. Little did I know that my "not applicable" single-seat crew was taking care of all of the coordination with external agencies I was too busy to handle myself.

No. 1 and 2 in the formation informed the supervisor of flying of my early return and emphasized the nature of the emergency and the need to get the fire trucks rolling immediately. No. 3 coordinated with approach control. He informed them I had an emergency and was on a 10-mile base for an opposite-direction approach and landing. As they handled the coordination, I performed all checklist items for a single-engine landing. I mentally prepared myself to emergency ground egress as fast as possible after landing and stopping the aircraft. My effective crew took about two minutes to collaborate with the personnel on the ground and coordinate the emergency landing. After the planning was complete, I switched to tower frequency and informed them my aircraft was still on fire and I was on a five-mile final for an opposite-direction landing.

The tower immediately cleared me to land. I reviewed my emergency landing data as I configured to land. With no hydraulic pressure in the right system, my speed brakes were unavailable, and I knew this would result in a longer landing distance. My right engine was still on fire as I approached the runway overrun. I focused on the landing and held the jet off the runway as long as I could to get to the slowest possible landing speed.

I lowered the nose to the runway and tapped the brakes to ensure they were working normally. I noticed the left side of the aircraft sink slightly, and, upon visual inspection, the left main tire had blown and was shooting sparks down the runway. I engaged my nose wheel steering to help keep the aircraft on the runway centre line. With the added drag of the blown tire, the aircraft came to a stop fairly quickly. My left main landing gear was now on fire, and my right engine was still burning unabated. It certainly was time to shut down the remaining engine, get out of the jet and let the firefighters go to work.

Thanks to No. 1 and 2, the fire trucks were immediately at my jet as it came to a stop. As I egressed the aircraft, the firefighters battled both fires for the next 15 minutes before finally extinguishing them.

Luckily, there were no injuries and the jet was eventually repaired.

Lessons Learned:

It was my crew's actions that kept me safe. We can all handle challenges in our single-seat fighters, but when time is at a premium, the thing that can keep us all safe is the delegation of duties, teamwork and solid crew resource management like that displayed by my four ship.

NOTES:

THE BEST $5 I'VE EVER LOST
A-10, 57TH WING, NELLIS AFB, NEV.

Major James Barlow, Spring 2012

It was an ideal Friday afternoon sortie, leading an instructor pilot-only continuation training four-ship formation to the bombing range in the A-10. The bet was standard at a quarter a bomb and a nickel a bullet.

We cruised out to the range at 100 feet above ground level. I checked onto range to begin our bombing and strafing. After my safe escape while climbing up for the second 45-degree high-altitude dive bomb, I noticed the jet was climbing slower than usual. I confirmed my speed brakes were in and checked the status of my engines. Both engines were well within the green arc on all parameters although No. 2's fan speed was 7 percent lower than No. 1's. I cycled the throttles to see where the engines settled in. Both engines were almost exactly parallel at all power settings, except at military power where the No. 2 fan speed was again low by 7 percent. With the engines both well within limits, I continued the mission and dropped my second 45- and two 30-degree dive bombs.

Next came my first 10-degree climb, and the No. 2 engine got my attention again. We were again at 100 feet, running in to pop up to 1,800 feet to execute a low-angle, high-drag delivery, but the jet just wasn't getting uphill like normal. I aborted my first pop and called "knock it off." I established an altitude stack and brought No. 2 into the high pattern while 3 and 4 continued to work low altitude.

There were no checklists or operations limits that applied to an engine when the only abnormal indication was 7 percent below No. 1 at military power setting on an engine where it's common to have needles that aren't parallel. I decided to bring the jet home and queried No. 2 for inputs. We agreed to maintain element integrity and returned to Davis-Monthan Air Force Base, Ariz., at medium altitude.

While en route, I reviewed all the Dash 1 checklists and in-flight guide pages that I would've reviewed if I'd actually experienced an engine failure. I also applied fighter resource management with No. 2 and asked if he could think of anything I might have missed. An experienced pilot flying as a wingman may have a bigger picture since he or she is removed from the emergency aircraft. In this case, No. 2 couldn't find anything missing, so we notified the supervisor of flying and I landed uneventfully via precautionary single-engine landing procedures.

After landing and engine shutdown, I had an engine specialist meet me at the jet to inspect the engine. I knew I'd made the right call when he told the production super, "Come look at this." As soon as it was my turn to climb up the ladder and look in the back of the engine, I was surprised to see the tip of every blade in the low-pressure turbine section was gone.

The extent of the damage resulted in a Class B mishap, but the investigation concluded the engine would have experienced a catastrophic failure if I'd continued the flight. Of course, I still had to pay for losing the bombing and gun events that I didn't accomplish due to recovering the jet early. However, I was able to save the Air Force and the A-10 community an engine that would live to fly and fight another day.

Lessons Learned:

The takeaway is that the jets are getting old and not every emergency will be neatly spelled out in the checklist. The jets will talk to you, but sometimes it's only a whisper.

It was the best $5 I've ever lost.

NOTES:

ROLL YOUR R'S TO ATC
F-16CJ, 77TH FIGHTER SQUADRON, SHAW AFB, S.C.

Captain Benjamin Lindsay, Spring 2012

So, there I was ... in a not-so-routine sortie with a requirement that few aviators enjoy – a projected 10.5-hour pond crossing in a cramped F-16CJ. Of the hundreds of potential malfunctions of a single engine, single-seat fighter, few require a "land as soon as possible" end result. That was the last thing on my mind after 10.1 hours of flight with numb legs and neck cramps.

What was on my mind at the time of the emergency procedure (EP) was trying to figure out what the Italian controller just said. Accent discrimination was not my forte as I scrambled to find a fix that sounded somewhat similar to the verbal garbage that my ear brain disconnect was trying to re-assemble. With maps of an unfamiliar country's airspace in hand and only a half-hour remaining, a sense of finality almost took over as I (No. 6 in the formation) was somewhat content to follow lead into Aviano AB, Italy. As soon as I folded the map and looked out at Mount Etna, an engine lube warning light promptly spoiled any chance of an uneventful recovery.

An engine lube warning light indicates the engine is running out of oil and the aircraft needs to be immediately put on any patch of concrete. Oil loss will inevitably result in engine seizure, at which point the aircraft would be a multi-million dollar multi-role glider.

Where do I divert? Do I jettison my tanks with all my gear and aircraft forms into the Mediterranean? I know nothing about Italy except for the red circles on my map indicating desired divert bases. New avionics upgrades include an emergency divert page which immediately increased my situational awareness, as well as my element lead saying, "Turn right and go to Grosseto!"

Easily visible was a strip of more than 8,000 feet that was soon within gliding distance. It was, indeed, Grosseto. With the throttle at idle and low key in the bag, I descended and attempted to get as much airfield info from my element lead as possible. I needed field elevation, tower frequency, cable locations, winds and ground support. Before I could utter those requests, No. 5 responded with all the info I needed to make a safe simulated flameout and landing. However, things got a little more complicated during the SFO. Communication broke down as I tried to comprehend the Italian-English tower controller. I thought about rolling my r's and enunciating with inflections based on memories of an aged pizza shop owner I knew. No luck ... just put it on the deck and use hand signals, I thought.

Approaching base key, the oil pressure dropped below Dash 1 limits and was decreasing slowly. To maintain hydraulics to land the aircraft in case of engine seizure, I activated my emergency power unit. Knowing that Grosseto has Eurofighters and would be familiar with hydrazine, my comfort level would've been increased except that I still couldn't understand the controllers. Thankfully my No. 5 was a Dutch exchange officer who helped to conclude this EP with a safe touchdown beyond raised cables.

After landing with wind direction details, due to hydrazine considerations, I pulled the jet on an adjacent taxiway to allow my element lead to land and the emergency response agencies to take care of me. Italian crash response units were very helpful in every regard, but I had to use a combination of Spanish and hand signals to communicate my intentions.

Lessons Learned:

Spending the night on an inflated G-suit in a 1960's Cold-War-era hardened aircraft shelter at a little-known airfield, I was able to reflect on the day's events. What if that same EP happened 250 nautical miles from Lajes Field, Portugal?

I started thinking about the ejection sequence and recovery procedures. What if the engine had seized? Would I have jettisoned my tanks and later had an interesting conversation with the ops group commander? I mulled over these and many more considerations with one thing in mind – mutual support is one of the most important mechanisms a fighter pilot has to combat adversity when things get ugly.

It's one thing to think about how I would handle the situation, but how would I help another flight mate in a similar situation? Reverse-engineering the problem with myself as the support asset, I spent time performing the oldest flight preparation technique in the book and one that I use in preparation for each flight to this day – chair flying. Perhaps I should have chair flown my Italian prior to launch.

NOTES:

INSIDIOUS DECOMPRESSION
B-52, 20TH BOMB SQUADRON, BARKSDALE AFB, LA.

Captain John M. Boos, July 2008

The sortie started out as your average training mission. It was a normal weekday at the 20th Bomb Squadron, Barksdale Air Force Base, in the battle-tested B-52H. We thoroughly briefed the mission the day before, ensuring all the paperwork was accomplished. The mission would take us to Lancer ATCCA for simulated weapons-activity training for an hour and a half, then off to rendezvous with a tanker for some aerial-refueling training, ending with us back home to beat up the pattern for a bit. A little nonstandard was that we would be flying with the vice wing commander, who was a radar navigator by trade, and it was also going to be a night sortie.

    We assembled at the squadron's front desk, where we exchanged paperwork with the duty dogs and received our step briefing. The bus got us to our jet with time for ground ops and on-time takeoff. During engine start, we had some mechanical issues, which ended up causing us to depart late. It wasn't a big deal, because we were scheduled for an hour and a half in the area and had some make-up time. The delay only cost us 30 minutes. The plan was to go into the area, do a couple of maneuvering gravity- bomb runs, and follow up with some simulated JDAM/CAS work.

The wing vice CC and I decided we would split seat time in the area. I had the radar navigator seat from takeoff until the first two gravity runs, and then I would turn it over to him for a gravity run and the JDAM/CAS work. I'd be playing the role of the joint terminal air controller, and had worked up challenging targets for the crew. The first series of targets I passed the crew was a multi-target run, which would require a max bank turn after the first weapon release to avoid the simulated threat, and achieve Launch Acceptability Region for the second weapon release. I passed the crew the target set, and they went to work on prosecuting the targets. During all of this, I was sitting in the instructor navigator seat, and it is a dark cockpit at night. The IN seat is on the lower deck of the BUFF, right above the crew-entrance hatch, surrounded by avionics gear, and the wonderful urinal tucked in the corner. I would have to compare it to sitting in a dark, noisy, smelly corner.

The crew did a great job taking the target information and other external information, and came up with a plan of attack. We made our push to the first of two targets, and everyone's full attention was on the task at hand. We struck our first target and then made a hard-break turn for target No. 2. In the turn, I started to feel a little short of breath; my view of the offense compartment started to go blurry. I convinced myself it was because of where I was sitting and that the hard turn was making my breathing a little shallow. After we rolled out, I was still feeling a little short of breath and having to breathe harder. We were about a minute out from releasing on the second target when the AC spoke up and asked if anyone else was feeling weird. He instinctively looked up at the cabin pressure gauge and realized the cabin pressure was climbing to meet us at FL340. He immediately called center for an emergency descent to FL180 and ordered the crew on 100 percent oxygen. The cabin pressure ended up meeting the aircraft altimeter at FL260 on our way down to FL180. Everyone got up on oxygen in a timely manner, and we decided it would be a good time to take the jet home. We stayed on oxygen all the way. The flight doc met us at the jet and gave us the OK to come off of O_2 after checking us for signs of decompression sickness.

Several different issues came into play with this incident. The biggest was the decompression of the aircraft. This was not a rapid decompression, but an insidious decompression — one that, in my mind, is much more dangerous. Being in the middle of a weapon run had caused the whole crew to have some form of channelized attention. The problem could not have happened at a more inopportune time in the sortie. The pilot asked if anyone had been feeling a little weird before we realized the problem. After we leveled off and talked about it, all crew members admitted they felt a little off before the pilot spoke up. This led me to wonder — if the pilot hadn't spoken up, would anyone have? I convinced myself the reasons I was feeling off was because I was sitting in the dark and we were in a max-bank turn, although the symptoms I felt were the same hypoxia symptoms I'd experienced in the chamber during physiological training. After all, although not an excuse, we only get chamber training once every five years. The symptoms are something, as aviators, we should be looking out for at all times. Something as small as insidious decompression is just waiting to rear its ugly head when we least expect it. Often, these small things can be fatal if not recognized and dealt with in the ways we're trained. That's why all our training as aircrews is so important. It can and will save our life and the lives of those flying with us, as long as we fall back on our training.

Lessons Learned:

Because we survived that incident to train and fight another day, I took away some valuable lessons from that sortie.

The first is to speak up if you're not feeling quite right about something. You may not have all the information at your disposal, but you may clue someone else in to something that's going on, putting a stop to the chain of events leading somewhere you don't want to go.

The other lesson I learned is to always fall back on your training. The Air Force spends a lot of money to train crew members so we can go out there and perform our jobs effectively and safely. The reason for our decompression issue was due to a failed part. These things will happen, and aviators must be prepared to deal with them correctly by using our training and constantly having our head on a swivel. Your life and those you fly with might just depend on it.

NOTES:

FULL THROTTLE OR GO HOME
KC-10, 32ND AIR REFUELING SQUADRON, MCGUIRE AFB, NEW JERSEY

Captain Bruce Holmgren, August 2008

We were cleared for takeoff from Al Dhafra Air Base, United Arab Emirates, on what should have been another routine day. The temperature was the same as it was every day — blistering hot. The aircraft weight was the same as it had been throughout the whole deployment — max allowable. As we finished our safety checks and set takeoff power, our KC-10 accelerated down the runway. As we gained altitude, raised the gear, switched radio frequencies, and started our first turn, the pilot flying called for climb power on the thrust rating computer, and the engines responded accordingly — or so we thought. As the auto throttles back out of takeoff power into climb power, you can normally anticipate an audible difference in the three engines as they slow ever so slightly; however, today was different. The small reduction in power became a large reduction as the thrust rating computer commanded the auto throttles to retard to the idle position. Our aircraft, full of jet fuel and at less than 2,000 feet above the ground, started to sink.

What came next was the result of excellent teamwork and hours of training. A quick scan showed that No. 1 and 3 (the wing engines) were approaching idle, while No. 2 was still producing max thrust. The pilot flying disengaged the auto throttles and returned the wing engine throttles to the approximate climb power position. With the No. 1 and 3 engines spooling up, an attempt to reduce No. 2 from takeoff to climb power identified our overall problem — it was binding. Our efforts resulted in reducing No. 2 RPM, but only enough to get it into the acceptable limits, not a percent more. There was no moving the throttle — it was full-throttle or go home with an engine shutdown. We opted for the latter.

At that point, our engine problem wasn't so bad. They were, after all, still producing thrust.

The three keys to any aircraft emergency, in order of importance, are to aviate, navigate and communicate. Thanks to our teamwork and training, we had taken care of the first step automatically, almost without thinking about it. We now had the aircraft under control and were safely climbing away from the ground. Now it was time to figure out where we were going and talk to the Emirate air traffic controller. We proceeded to the designated fuel dump area where we "adjusted our gross weight" in order to return for a landing. Twenty minutes later, we were light enough to land and ready to initiate the checklist that would lead us to an engine shutdown in flight. Again, teamwork from all four crew members resulted in a successful fuel dump and engine shutdown. Following what seemed like endless coordination (on four different radios, simultaneously), we were ready for our final approach. We had experienced enough fun and excitement for one day, but as luck would have it, we weren't done yet.

Every pilot knows that your sortie isn't over until your engines are shut down and the chocks are in place. Today, Murphy and his silly law took yet another opportunity to drive that point home. As the pilot flying touched down, he began to lower the nose to the runway and reached for the thrust reversers — a well-engrained habit pattern in the KC-10 community. What we didn't count on was that the No. 2 engine throttle would be inconveniently in the way of the No. 1

and 3 thrust reversers. Now that we're trying to stop with a throttle still in the takeoff position, our takeoff warning horn was making us deafer by the second. This was not a routine day. Were we done? Of course not. We blew a tire.

Finally, luck was on our side. The tire that blew was from the center gear, so there was no pull to either side. In fact, we didn't even feel it blow. It was all thanks to an observation from the ground emergency services, quick coordination with the control tower, and an expediting maintenance team to secure the tire and get us off the runway. Once we got the call about the blown tire, we were a little surprised. We made a conscious effort to not make a bad situation worse. We had previously discussed runway length, our operative systems, and that there was no need to get on the brakes early — so we didn't. We later learned from maintenance that the blown tire was a result from an anti-skid malfunction — with no correlation to our emergency or crew actions.

Lessons Learned:

As an avid football fan, I've had my share of experience with "Monday-morning quarterbacking." Looking back on the incident, there are a few things I'd like to highlight.

1. Don't allow yourself to get complacent. There are no such things as routine sorties. With our aging aircraft, high ops tempo, and ever-changing environment, things will go wrong; you have to be ready for anything.

2. Take your training seriously. In the KC-10, we don't practice engine-out ops in the jet — only in the simulator. Thanks to great sim training and lessons from experienced sim instructors, we were well-prepared and our emergency was fairly uneventful. I consider any emergency a success when you can walk away from it and say, "Yeah, it was just like the sim."

3. Don't underestimate the importance of teamwork and crew resource management. Throughout the whole flight and back on the ground, our flight engineer and boom operator played crucial roles in safely recovering the aircraft.

4. Remember Murphy's Law is always in effect; consider every possible situation (i.e., better coordination with thrust reversers on landing roll and anticipating the need to find the takeoff warning horn circuit breaker). Though it's impossible to think of every scenario, if you can bind your mind at full throttle, your training will take over, and the rest will come naturally.

NOTES:

SHAPING THE EJECTION DECISION
F-15, 80TH FLYING TRAINING WING, SHEPPARD AFB, TEXAS

Major Jeffrey Galloway, Fall 2011

I was on the second of three legs on a benign, solo cross-country flight when I had a hydraulic malfunction that forced me to do an alternate gear extension and take an approach-end cable. I ran the checklist, declared the emergency and coordinated with the base of landing in accordance with the numerous emergency simulators I'd done. Everything went as expected until touchdown when the left main gear collapsed, and I started skidding down the runway. I immediately recognized there was something wrong.

It took about a second to recognize the left main gear had collapsed, and the plane was settling on the external fuel tanks. About the time I analysed the problem, I saw the approach-end cable pass in my peripheral vision followed by a moderate deceleration and an increasing drift to the left despite engaging the barrier in the center of the runway. I was unable to successfully counter the drift due to the previous hydraulic failure and lack of normal brakes and steering. It was then that I realized the drift was turning into a rapid left turn, and I was going to depart the prepared surface.

I fell back on my training as I was contemplating an ejection when I remembered the 100-knot technique as a decision point on when to eject and when to stay with the aircraft. Since I was rapidly decelerating through 100 knots, I decided to stay with the aircraft and ride it out. The aircraft quickly came to a stop 400 feet past the barrier, 200 feet off the prepared surface and almost 90 degrees heading off from the runway. I performed an emergency ground egress and ran away from the accident without a scratch.

This sounds like a story of proper decision making and successfully relying on training, but it's what I didn't know at the time that almost killed me. It wasn't until later that I found out my left wingtip, which was dragging on the ground, missed a large grate in the infield of the runway by a foot. They said I wasn't going fast enough for the wingtip to shear off, but I was going fast enough for the aircraft to spin and roll. I made the wrong decision and lived to tell about it.

The 100-knot technique is still valid because I don't want to go three wheeling at a high rate of speed across the infield. I still use this technique, but only if I'm rolling on all gears, not sliding sideways and not going to hit something that extends above ground level. I'd rather trust the ejection seat and life support equipment than roll the dice on crossing the unfamiliar ground of an airfield in a configuration that won't allow you to roll over small obstacles. This technique is also supported by another mishap where the aircraft was sliding off the runway sideways. Since the speed of the aircraft was less than 100 knots, the aircrew stayed in it. When the aircraft departed the prepared surface, the gear dug in; the aircraft rolled and luckily landed right side up sparing the crew.

This natural hesitation and reluctance to eject is not only confined to ground ejections. Another mishap reshaped my airborne ejection decision. Aircrew can tell you the minimum controlled and uncontrolled ejection altitudes of their specific seat, but how do you apply them? I was taught if the aircraft is not recovering to controlled flight when you approach the minimum uncontrolled ejection altitude, then eject. I had to adjust my thinking after a mishap where the

SHAPING THE EJECTION DECISION

aircraft was recovering when it was approaching the minimum uncontrolled ejection altitude, then it went out of control again below the minimum uncontrolled ejection altitude.

Making judgments about why the aircraft is out of control and basing your assumptions on aircraft recovery on that judgment is risking your life if you descend through the minimum uncontrolled ejection altitude. After this revelation, I adjusted my ejection decision to being recovered, not just recovering when approaching the uncontrolled ejection altitude.

These first two examples require split-second decision making which is why we try to make the decision prior to flight. But even in more benign situations during controlled flight, we don't want to make the decision to eject and want to save the aircraft. I've seen warnings in the Dash-1 aircraft manual along the lines of "Do not delay ejection below the minimum controlled ejection altitude in futile attempts to start the engines or for reasons that may commit you to an unsafe ejection." Despite this, aircrews repeatedly violate this warning. Since my hands are most likely on the throttle and stick at the time of the event, I can quickly attempt to recover the aircraft to sustained flight using boldface emergency procedures. If this attempt doesn't work resulting in immediate positive indications of returning to sustained flight and I'm unable to zoom the aircraft above the minimum controlled ejection altitude, then it's time to eject.

Lessons Learned:

Every second you delay in making the decision to eject, you risk your life. It's not the time to trust your luck. It's time to jettison the aircraft and trust the modern ejection seats which have an excellent survival rate ... if you eject in the envelope.

NOTES:

COMPOUND EMERGENCIES
C-130 HERCULES, OPERATIONAL INFORMATION WITHHELD

Name withheld by request, Fall 2011

There I was, flying in the right seat of my C-130 coming home from the AOR. The trip to the sand box had gone smoothly. After spending a night downrange, we loaded up to start the journey back. What we didn't suspect at the time was that this would be the day we'd fall behind schedule and be tested in a way no one on the crew had been before.

I was still relatively new to my squadron having only been there approximately six months straight out of the schoolhouse. While we were flying somewhere over the Mediterranean Sea, someone noticed an engine oil low light. In my short career, I'd already seen a couple of prop low oil lights but never an engine oil low light. From the light, our eyes quickly shifted up to the oil gauges to see which engine was having the issue, and it was obvious when we saw that No. 4 was completely empty! Normally, the light will come on at approximately four gallons remaining, which told us this engine must have lost its oil very quickly. After the shutdown, we discussed our options as a crew and checked the regulations. We were enroute to Royal Air Force

Mildenhall, U.K., and having maintenance there and a favorable weather forecast, we decided to continue our trip. However, if you've been flying very long, you know that forecasts aren't always spot on.

Crossing the Mediterranean, we were finally back over land and closing in on the Alps. We were at 16,000 mean sea level (MSL) when the weather started to creep up to our level. From our forecast, we were only supposed to have light icing up to 14,000 MSL. As we started entering the weather, it became apparent that the icing forecast was a little "off." The Hercules has excellent anti-icing capabilities ... assuming they work as advertised. By this time, we were well over the mountains and trying to climb up and out of the icing level. We then noticed neither the No. 2 engine inlet anti-ice nor the spinner de-ice was working. As the ice building up on the inlet was quickly turning into a large block of ice, we started to have visions of that engine ingesting that block.

We were still over the mountains and couldn't yet descend and oh, by the way, weren't doing a very good job of climbing out of the icing either. We eventually got down to about 130 knots indicated airspeed (KIAS) with maximum power set on the remaining engines, and we just popped out of the weather. We were basically hanging on the props as we skidded along the top of the clouds. We were out of the ice but still not having a good time. Our maintainers in the back were all awake by this time and were frantically running back and forth from wing to wing trying to see what was going on out on the engines. Other maintainers were up front with the engineer trying to figure out why the anti icing was only partially working. Our engineer accidentally received a large shock while trying to troubleshoot anti-ice issues back in the electrical equipment.

To top things off, we also received a No. 1 prop fluxing out of limits that would not correct! To recap, we had one engine shutdown, another in shutdown condition and another that could ingest a block of ice at any moment. We were flying at 130 KIAS just out of reach of the icing, the mountains were still below and there was a whole crew of maintainers who you could say was a bit "concerned."

Before things got too much worse, we finally cleared the mountains and made a high-speed descent through the icing. We found the closest piece of suitable pavement we could to put the plane down. The aircraft commander elected to not shut down the No. 1 engine with the prop malfunction. Due to the greater emergencies we were dealing with, he decided it wasn't worth shutting that one down and ending up on two engines. We landed uneventfully.

Lessons Learned:

The best takeaway for me in this event was dealing with compound emergencies. We had several different problems going on at once, and we really had to prioritize them. It was a great example of the old adage of "aviate, navigate and communicate."

We had to decide what the greatest risk was at each particular phase in the sequence of emergencies and adjust appropriately. In the end, I think we handled a complex situation reasonably well as a crew, and I don't think I would've done anything differently had I been in the left seat.

NOTES:

SAFE LANDINGS

CV-22B OSPREY, 36TH MAINTENANCE SQUADRON, ANDERSEN AFB, GUAM

Senior Master Sergeant Quintus Woods, Summer 2011

I was the production superintendent in the 71st Aircraft Maintenance Unit responsible for five CV-22B Osprey tilt-rotor aircraft. I had been in this position for about 1.5 years and had more than nine years of experience in the aircraft. In all my years working with the Osprey, I had never experienced what we were in store for that night. I was working the swing shift and during the turnover to the mid shift production superintendent, we got the call, "Osprey 4 MOC aircraft is 20 minutes out with an unsafe nose-landing-gear condition."

Immediately, we both jumped into action. The mid-shift super started running the emergency action checklist, while I went into the hangar and quickly assigned specific tasks to the maintainers. Luckily, we had extra people due to both swing and mid-shifts at work. After all the tasks were assigned, I ran over to the 71st Special Operations Squadron's operations desk. There we made contact with the aircraft commander. We discussed our plan of action using the emergency-action checklist as a guide.

The plan was to have the aircraft hover at the hover pad, while two crew chiefs verified the nose-landing gear was down and locked. Once the aircraft arrived, the two crew chiefs tried their best to get under the aircraft that was hovering just overhead. They tried two attempts, and on the second try, one of the crew chiefs injured his left wrist when the wind sent him cartwheeling about 15 feet down the flightline. After that happened, we realized how dangerous it was going to be to inspect the landing gear. I made the call to pull the crew chiefs to prepare for a mattress landing.

I assigned a crew to set up the mattress-landing area. This involved strapping down two stacks of regular twin-sized mattresses using tie downs to the designated landing spot. They grabbed our pre staged mattress-landing trailer and set up the spot in slightly more than seven minutes.

Again, I went to the operations desk and contacted the aircraft commander, and we went over the plan for landing this 36,000-pound aircraft on some mattresses. The crew chiefs were in place, and I jumped into the truck and went out to ensure everything was set for the landing. The aircraft hovered over to the spot. The crew chiefs battled the rotor wash, while they marshaled the aircraft down and landed it safely on the ground. It was a huge relief to see the aircraft resting safely on the mattresses.

We accomplished the first mattress landing in the history of the Osprey. I was very proud of the outstanding performance of the 71 AMU maintainers.

This was an amazing task that, outside of a minor wrist injury, was performed flawlessly. This is the day we had been training for, but until you have to actually perform the task, you can only guess how things will go. The men and women of the 71 AMU were ready. Without training, things could've gone very badly. Our efforts helped save the lives of the six aircrew members that were on the aircraft that night.

Lessons Learned:

From our experience, we were able to identify some areas for improvement. From a safety standpoint, for all future mattress landings, no one was allowed under a hovering Osprey to verify the landing gear. The maintenance crew would go directly to the mattress landing spot. Also, we received some concerns from the aircrew. The crew chiefs were too close when they were bringing the aircraft in. The last thing we did was add a reference line for the aircraft commander to identify and use to help land the aircraft.

Overall, this was a safe and successful landing. All six subsequent Osprey mattress landings the 71st encountered were successfully performed and can be directly attributed to safety-conscious maintainers and their continued pursuit of excellence.

NOTES:

NO IFE'S

KC-135, AIR REFUELER, 99 ARS, ROBINS AFB, GA

Captain Devin K. Pietrzak, April 2008

As I was sitting around a table during flight debrief after my last flight in 2006, I began to think about how, after nearly nine years of flying, I'd always been able to walk away from the jet, knowing that the mission was complete and another safe flight had been completed. Many of you might sit back and not think much about that statement, but what wasn't mentioned was that during all my flights, I've also been able to say that I've never experienced an in-flight emergency.

To give perspective on my aviation career, I started out going through navigator training at Pensacola Naval Air Station, Fla. As part of my training, the program consisted of eight flights at the controls of the T-34C, followed by four more rides in the Turbo Mentor, riding in the back seat. After this phase, the class would track to a more specialized phase with Tanker/Airlift, completing training at Randolph Air Force Base, Texas. I chose to PCS to Randolph and completed my training in the T-43, a variant of the Boeing 737. After training, I picked up my first assignment to Robins Air Force Base, Ga., as most KC-135 navigators were assigned there or McConnell Air Force Base, Kan. After a three-month training tour at Altus Air Force Base, Okla., I finally made it to Georgia. Before arriving there, I amassed more than 150 hours of flying time, free of any emergencies, even minor system interruptions.

During my next three and a half years and 500+ hours as a KC-135R navigator, I never experienced an IFE. Those years included multiple deployments, several overseas trips in support of Coronets, many joint readiness exercises, and hundreds of local training missions. There were minor cases of pressurization problems, and an electrical issue once or twice, but nothing preventing us from finishing our mission and landing. The crew debrief typically concluded the same way, as all crew members agreed that another safe mission was complete.

About five years into my flying career and four more into my current position, what happened? Pilot training. I was lucky enough to be selected for SUPT, and happily left for Columbus for another year of Air Education & Training Command and CONUS flying training. After flying the T-34C, I knew that tracking Heavy/Tanker was the right move for me. My previous experience as a navigator coming from a crew airplane, made me realize how nice it was having extra sets of eyes on the instruments and having other crew members backing up all phases of the mission. When it came time to choose the aircraft I wanted to fly, I chose to go right back into the KC-135R at Robins. So, after a third trip to Altus Air Force Base, three months of flying, and another 200+ hours of AETC, I arrived back at Robins Air Force Base. Again, the training was free from minor system issues and IFEs.

OIF and OEF were still in full swing, so qualification training was expeditious, and out the door I went to deploy. Our aircraft was starting to see more maintenance issues, with constant heavyweight takeoffs and hot sandy conditions. Still, after more than 500 hours of flying during my first two deployments, no IFE.

Four Altus tours and four flying deployments behind me, I sat around the debrief table, awaiting the same words from all my crew members on how the flight was fine, and everything was done safely. However, after almost nine years of flying, I heard the comment that must have passed through one ear and out the other when I was a co-pilot and navigator. A crew member said that during the briefing for the flight, we glossed over the mission too quickly and spent too much time discussing EPs. This was a shock to me, because through all crew positions I've flown in, I've never had an issue with the briefing on emergency procedures. One point to consider was that this mission wasn't typical. Our Special Missions office accomplished the mission planning and briefed the crew on that night's mission. After the specialized briefing, I felt that I offered up as much time as needed for the navigator's personal brief that included more detailed items and crew resource management issues with four-person operations. After all these years, ONE crew member said, "Too much time on EP briefing." I started to question myself. Did the office that briefed our specialized mission not brief enough? Did I not give ample time to the mission navigator to clear up any gray areas?

I dug deeper into how I brief for local training sorties. Nine years without an IFE! Was I spending too much time on briefing crew actions during an emergency? I eventually took this question on my drive home. This allowed me to think more clearly without interruptions, and I later came to my conclusion. First, I considered the several variations that our crew brief can go through, depending on each unique refueling mission. Next, I looked at how we brief during deployments, when we fly with the same crew members and begin to understand how each one deals with in-flight situations. When flying with hard crews, briefs tend to shorten, with the understanding that non-mission specific actions remain the same as the previous flight. This is vastly different from during training programs, when many flight members are in the early learning phase, and repetition is vital, making sure everyone learns how to effectively take care of issues together as a crew. This is what we call a form of CRM. Last are local training missions. For the KC-135, crews consist of a minimum of three, but have consisted of more than 10 to complete training. These briefings are then tailored to meet specific crew and mission training. That night of my last flight, we had eight crew members on the aircraft, and I felt confident that all primary crew members understood the mission. Eight is a large crew for the KC-135, and it's very important that everyone know their role during an emergency.

The mission wasn't perfect, but we completed all training and didn't experience an IFE. During debrief, we discussed specific issues we had during the flight, and I felt satisfied with the length of my briefing covering EPs before we stepped.

Lessons Learned:

So, why after nine years and not a single IFE, am I writing this story? I wanted to tell my story to all crew members out there to remain confident in their briefings.

Make sure you feel comfortable with how the briefing is being led, and if you have an issue during the brief, speak up about it. Ultimately, make sure the crew is prepared. Remain confident in your actions and don't get complacent. Mission planning and briefings are there to ensure that happens. Like the old saying goes, "Plan to fly, and fly the plan." I'm confident that if our crew were to encounter an IFE, we would've been prepared and would've handled the emergency properly.

Always be prepared and ready for that unexpected problem. Don't become lazy in your flying, because you never know — today may be the day your EP training is put to the test!

NOTES:

EMERGENCY COMMS
A-10 THUNDERBOLT, OPERATIONAL INFORMATION WITHHELD

Name withheld by request, September 2008

While leading a two-ship of A-10s for a close air support training mission, I descended the formation below the MOA for a simulated troops-in-contact situation. As I came off target for my last pass at approximately 1,000 feet and almost 90 degrees of bank, the cockpit started to fill with smoke. I immediately rolled wings level, started a climb and made a knock-it-off call, and informed the flight of my smoke-and-fume situation.

The smoke had a toxic smell, burned my eyes, and was becoming very intense. I quickly ran the smoke-and-fumes elimination checklist from memory, but it wasn't getting any better. The smoke made it difficult to see in or out of the cockpit.

My wingman confirmed that I was still wings level and headed in the right direction. I informed him that I had run the smoke-and-fumes elimination checklist and the smoke wasn't dissipating. He asked me to confirm one of my switches and he was spot on. I had accidentally put a switch in the wrong position when applying the smoke-and-fumes elimination procedures. Once corrected, the smoke quickly cleared, but the odor was still intense, and my eyes were watering from the fumes.

Now was my first chance to scan the cockpit, and I noticed the No. 1 engine oil was below limits. I brought the throttle to idle in accordance with the checklist and was able to get the oil within limits. I had my wingman read the oil system malfunction checklist to ensure I hadn't overlooked anything. Then, I declared my emergency with Approach Control, switched to tower to coordinate my arrival and ensure the emergency information was correctly relayed from Approach. While I did this, I had my wingman coordinate with the SOF. He informed him of the emergency, the checklists run and current status and game plan. I landed uneventfully from a straight-in approach.

The lesson I learned from the above situation was the importance of good communication during an emergency. As flight lead, I quickly communicated my problem following the knock-it-off call and again when I discovered the oil was out of limits. This allowed my wingman the opportunity to offer better mutual support and to help think through my emergency. Instead of struggling with the smoke and possibly jettisoning the canopy, I kept the wingman in the loop. I didn't rush to declare an emergency and avoided multiple questions from ATC that I wasn't ready to answer. Lastly, I reduced my task load by having the wingman coordinate with the SOF, while I spoke with tower.

The communication from my wingman was outstanding. He initially stayed off the radios and allowed me to work the problem. Later, when it was appropriate, he wasn't afraid to offer a suggestion when I told him the smoke wasn't clearing. His input was critical in handling the emergency. When I told him I was bringing the engine to idle for the low oil pressure, he again kept quiet and just thought through the situation. His thorough radio call to the SOF included my initial indications, checklists run and results, and finally a game plan.

The communication from ATC and SOF was minimal, just like

you would want. My calls to ATC and the wingman's call to the SOF provided all the information they needed to do their jobs. This was important because they have a responsibility to assist in an emergency, and if they're kept in the dark, chances are they're going to start asking questions. And it will probably be at the worst possible time. You, in the emergency aircraft, have now lost some control of your situation. It's much better to push information to outside agencies than have them continually trying to pull information from you.

Lessons Learned:

While this mishap proved to be an example of good communication, I've also experienced really poor examples of communication during emergency situations. Take, for example, those times when you inform the RSU controller that you have an emergency, so you can enter their pattern or get a chase ship, but get way more than you expected. The controller feels obligated to question you on every step of the checklist. Then they start offering suggestions for recovering the aircraft. SOFs can be guilty of this also. This comm jamming can be very distracting, reducing the pilot's situational awareness and overall hampering the situation.

The exact opposite of the above examples can also happen. The SOF or RSU controller that does nothing and confirms nothing can have equally poor outcomes. Let's assume there's an emergency in progress, but the pilot hasn't communicated anything to outside agencies. In this case, the SOF or RSU then needs to start pulling information and not be so passive. If they recognize the emergency is being poorly handled, they should speak up. They can't assume just because it's a qualified pilot that everything is being handled correctly. The SOF and RSU have the advantage of being ground speed zero to make more rational decisions, and they also have all the necessary publications.

As with any communications, you should always strive for C4 comm ... clear, concise, correct, and cool; especially during an emergency. Clearly and concisely state your emergency. Correctly communicate to the SOF what systems you've lost and what indications you have.

What does the emergency pilot expect from their flight lead/wingman, RSU or SOF? What's expected of the emergency pilot? When does too little or too much communication detract from handling the emergency situation? You ask a single-seat fighter pilot what they want to hear from their wingman and some still expect nothing but "Lead, you're on fire." So what's the answer? It depends. The difference between good and bad communication during an emergency situation can be very small, but the outcome can be enormously different.

NOTES:

NO. 2 ENGINE BLEED AIR LEAK
E-3, 962ND AIRBORNE AIR CONTROL SQUADRON, 3RD OPERATIONS GROUP, ELMENDORF AFB, ALASKA

Yukla 21 Crew, June 2007

On June 26, 2007, the crew departed from home station on a pilot proficiency sortie. As the crew descended into Eielson Air Force Base for practice pattern work, they began noticing several seemingly unrelated irregularities, such as popped circuit breakers and engine gauge malfunctions.

Recalling a previous E-3 Class B mishap, they astutely, quickly and correctly analyzed the problem as a serious No. 2 engine bleed air leak. Despite that there were no checklist procedures to assess or handle this type of situation, they correctly elected to shut down the engine and immediately return to home station.

This near-duplicate malfunction occurred four years ago, resulting in more than $700,000 in damages. The decisive actions of the crew of Yukla 21 prevented an imminent engine fire, limited damages, and ensured the safe return of a multimillion dollar aircraft.

NOTES:

IMMINENT ENGINE FAILURE
F-16CM, 85TH TEST AND EVALUATION SQUADRON, EGLIN AIR FORCE BASE, FLA.

Captain Gregory Barasch, March 2008

On March 11, 2008, Captain Barasch was No. 2 in a two-ship, F-16CM operational test mission to drop two inert 2,000-pound laser guided bombs. Immediately after takeoff, Capt. Barasch noted an "engine lube-low" light, indicating the engine's oil level was below 40 percent.

Quickly determining that engine failure was imminent, he established a one-to-one glide ratio, despite a low cloud ceiling. Capt. Barasch scanned his engine instruments and noted that the oil pressure was reading below normal and steadily decreasing. He immediately began a climb to establish a one-one glide ratio back to Eglin.

He elected to delay jettisoning the two inert bombs and two 370-gallon fuel tanks because of his proximity to the densely populated beach resort area of Destin, Fla. and base housing.

This decision prevented possible damage to people and property. Flying a simulated flameout approach, he successfully recovered the aircraft. Capt. Barasch's exceptional flying skills and situational awareness allowed him to safely recover a high value test aircraft and prevent injury to personnel or property damage.

NOTES:

NO O2 AT 41,000 FEET
F-16, 14TH FIGHTER SQUADRON, MISAWA AB, JAPAN

Major Darrell F. Thomas, July 2007

Decisive action during a flight emergency on July 27, 2007.

About 30 minutes into the sortie, during a climb to 41,000 feet, Maj. Thomas started to feel a tingling sensation, and immediately recognized the symptoms of hypoxia. He quickly checked his oxygen pressure regulator and discovered he had a no-flow indication.

Maj. Thomas started an immediate emergency descent, declared an in-flight emergency, and safely recovered the aircraft. Soon thereafter, maintenance personnel discovered the supply hose at the bottom of the oxygen regulator had become detached, thereby making any chance of acquiring desperately needed oxygen impossible.

Maj. Thomas' professionalism, recognition of hypoxic symptoms, and understanding of the severe danger he faced, coupled with knowledge of the F-16 systems, allowed him to avert a potential Class A flight mishap. His actions ultimately resulted in minimal mission impact.

NOTES:

MISSILE WARNING

C-130, 61ST AIRLIFT SQUADRON, 643RD AIR GROUP, LITTLE ROCK AFB, ARKANSAS

Torque 88 Crew, April 2008

Outstanding achievements during a flight emergency on April 18, 2007.

During departure from Sharana Landing Zone, Afghanistan, to Bagram Air Base, Afghanistan, the crew received a missile warning at only 200 feet above the ground. While performing the appropriate actions in response to the threat, the No. 3 engine flamed out at only two knots above minimum control speed. The razor-sharp crew expertly handled this critical emergency, while simultaneously scanning for additional threats and avoiding dangerously high terrain.

The crew brought this emergency to a successful conclusion by restarting the engine, performing a climb to a safe en route altitude, and returning to home station. The investigation revealed a piece of a turbine blade had catastrophically failed and caused the malfunction.

The quick reaction and excellent crew coordination enabled the safe return of 22 passengers, six crew members, and a $30 million aircraft.

NOTES:

CATASTROPHIC ENGINE FAILURE
STUDIES AND ANALYSIS SQUADRON, RANDOLPH AIR FORCE BASE, TEXAS

Major Kent S. Currie, March 2008

On March 5, 2008, while flying a distinguished visitor indoctrination sortie, the single-engine aircraft experienced significant engine vibrations followed immediately by a master warning, indicating imminent catastrophic engine failure.

Demonstrating outstanding situational awareness and system knowledge, Maj. Currie immediately terminated maneuvering and initiated a return to Randolph. While en route, the engine failed.

Due to his quick and deliberate actions at the onset of the vibrations, Maj. Currie had achieved sufficient altitude for an engine-out glide into the field. Displaying remarkable poise and airmanship, Maj. Currie deftly completed all emergency procedures in full accordance with technical publications while manoeuvring the engine-out aircraft into position for landing. His emergency was further complicated by a malfunction of the flaps, forcing time-critical energy management decisions while in close proximity to the ground.

Demonstrating remarkable flying skill and unflappable concentration, Maj. Currie compensated for the flap malfunction and continued his flawless execution of a forced landing to runway 14R.

The quick and deliberate actions of Maj. Currie saved a valuable $4.5 million asset and the lives of two crew members.

NOTES:

CHAPTER 6
COMPLACENCY

"Test pilots don't take as much risk as fighter pilots. Test flying is very controlled, with engineers supporting every mission….. Being a test pilot was probably the safest flying I ever did!"

Colonel Tom Henricks, USAF

HASTE MAKES WASTE
F-16 VIPER, OPERATIONAL INFORMATION WITHHELD

Name withheld by request, Nov 2008

You've probably heard it more than once from an instructor, "When you allow yourself to get out of your habit pattern, watch out!" Anyone who has stepped late or stepped to a spare pressed for time knows this truth.

Rushing to the Viper for a complex SEAD ride, the foremost thing on my mind was not my walk around. Instead, I was trying to grasp this sortie in my budding, non-mission-ready mind. I soon discovered that Murphy was working against me again, with a jet parked on the far side of the ramp. After checking the forms, I sped around the aircraft flying through the checks. What I failed to notice could have cost the Air Force a valuable asset and ended up costing many man-hours and dollars.

After a normal start, I began to perform the check on the secondary engine control by running up the PW- 229 engine. I then followed up with a check of the emergency power unit by running up the engine to 80 percent again. When the test failed, I ran the engine up to the max of 85 percent for the check. The EPU check again failed, so I called for a *redball* and prepared to shut down the aircraft for this no-go item. After shutdown, I headed back to the squadron without performing another walk around, disappointed that there wasn't a spare available.

Ten minutes later in the squadron, I overheard words that made me sick. Maintenance found an ingested intake cover in my tail number for that go. At first I thought that it wasn't my aircraft; there was no way I would have missed that. Yet, there was no disputing that it was me. I knew that I would soon get an education on how maintenance pulls a motor from an F-16.

How did I miss something so obvious? I was in disbelief. Every time I do a walk around, I physically poke my cranium into the intake to look for FOD. Every time, except this once. I walked quickly across the nose checking the AOA probes and never noticed the intake. I also allowed myself to become accustomed to seeing the intake covers in place as I walked up to the aircraft I was about to fly. Sometimes the crew chiefs, probably wanting to protect the engine until the last moment, leave the plug in the intake. I allow the crew chief to remove the cover during my walk around, rather than remove it immediately myself. This time, I missed it, and the crew chief missed it.

It was fortunate this mistake didn't cost more. I ground-aborted the aircraft for an unrelated reason. The engine showed no abnormal indications during start or during the higher RPM checks. If I had taxied and attempted to run up to mil power at takeoff, engine damage would have been much worse, and the consequences of an abort or even a takeoff with a damaged engine could have been catastrophic.

I spent a lot of time with the maintainers and engine troops after this incident. Most of the vinyl and foam plug disintegrated and blew through the bypass and out the back of the engine. Portions of the vinyl stuck to the fan and melted on. Fortunately, damage was minor. The mistake, however, remains major.

How did I make this mistake?

Let me say that there are no excuses for an incomplete walk around. It's true that some of the responsibility falls on the crew chief, but I'm the one taking the aircraft, and it's a big red cover ... c'mon. However, certain smaller factors caused me to miss an obvious discrepancy.

1. I didn't put my mind in the right state at step. My mind was on my role as wingman in the sortie. That's exactly where it should have been, but not at the expense of the "here and now." I didn't prioritize the tasks at hand. Ground ops took a back seat to tasks that wouldn't happen for another hour.

2. I'd allowed myself to become accustomed to seeing an engine cover while doing my walk around. This is something that should always look out of place on an aircraft ready to fly. If there are pins or covers present that shouldn't be there, the first priority should be to have the crew chief remove those "remove before flight" items, or do it myself. A final "big picture" check in front of the aircraft to check for obvious discrepancies before jumping up the ladder would have saved me on this one.

3. I was rushed from the brief to step to engine start. Despite the need to start and taxi on time, it isn't worth a second-rate preflight. Nobody in my squadron would have held me in disdain for taking the time I needed for safe and effective checks.

4. I got out of my habit pattern. Physically peering down the intake of the engine was a habit I'd had since RTU, as was a final walk in front of the aircraft to check for big-picture discrepancies. I deleted those habits that day, and Murphy was there to take a chunk out of my ego and my engine.

Lessons Learned:

When your good habit patterns are broken, watch out. Do a mental inventory and checks as necessary to rewind and recheck. It may take more time, but it might save much more.

NOTES:

NO CLEARANCE LANDING
C-130 HERCULES, 71ST RESCUE SQUADRON, MOODY AFB, GA.

Captain Tyler Fisk, Summer 2012

There we were – a C-130 crew who had just wrapped up the third flight in the AOR and were headed "home" for the night. Little did we know we'd be talking with the commander in a couple of hours and possibly getting sent home a few months short of our planned return date.

Let me set the scene.

I was a relatively experienced navigator heading out on my third deployment. The aircraft commander was on his first deployment in the left seat but had deployed several times before, as had the co-pilot, flight engineer and loadmasters. Overall, we were a combat-seasoned crew. We'd flown the aircraft from the states uneventfully and were getting settled into our new digs. We'd all deployed to this particular location in Southwest Asia several times and knew the airspace, controllers, flying ops, ground ops, parking spots and chow hall extremely well. We even spoke the local language with proper dialect. In case you can't read between the lines, this foreshadows complacency in the first degree.

We'd flown on a day schedule for the past week and already flown several missions. We all seemed to pick up where we left off a few months prior, and it felt like we never left theater. On this particular mission, we got quick turned to a night line and went back into the box. We hacked our 12-hour day and returned to base for termination. It was about 3 a.m., and we got handed off from center to approach. We were the only aircraft in the terminal area and started to set up for the visual approach. The last thing any of us remembers was being at 3,000 feet above mean sea level. Then we heard, "HERKY 31, you land with no clearance! You no clearance to land!" This guy was seriously upset.

After you feel your heart fall to your feet and the crew members look at each other and think, Did we not?... it occurs to you to push up the throttles and call a go-around. That did not happen. Instead, we put the Herk in reverse, got on the brakes and taxied clear of the active runway to finish talking with the tower.

The American liaison got on the tower frequency and told us not to worry about it; it was partly their fault. We briefly considered going with the thought, Freebie.

No one saw; no one's the wiser. Instead, we parked the plane, went into ops and fessed up our mistake.

The night operations officer sent us to bed, and we reported back down to the squadron a couple of hours later to sort out the matter. Things did get ironed out, and we finished our deployment. We were much more vigilant for it.

Lessons Learned:

It's worth taking a look at some of the lessons learned and what you can take away from our errors.

The overriding culprit in this scenario was complacency. Just because we had flown this identical approach to this base a hundred times doesn't preclude us from basic airmanship. GET CLEARANCE TO LAND. As a crew, we had become so used to the sequence of events in this portion of the flight that we forgot the basics. The entire segment from 3,000 feet to touchdown was a blank. It was like driving your car when you're too tired, and the next thing you know you're pulling into your driveway. Except this was a multimillion-dollar, 100,000-pound piece of metal.

The scariest part is that not one crew member even remembered running the checklists, configuring the airplane, getting the hand off to tower and doing the other parts of an approach, such as putting the aircraft in a safe position to land. We did it all subconsciously. Think about this: If we weren't doing these things, do you think we were visually clearing for other traffic, monitoring systems or looking at the runway for other hazards like trucks or wildlife? Unfortunately, the answer is no. Thankfully, there was no one else on final approach or taking the runway at the time.

There were other compounding factors, like being quick turned and over confident. The bottom line was there is no excuse for what happened, and we are all better aviators now for that experience.

One of many take-aways I learned from the experience was the 3 C's: Checklist, Clearance and Configuration.

If you ask yourself these three questions or verbalise them to the crew every time you set up for a landing, chances are you might just save yourself some time in front of the man or a trip to an early grave.

NOTES:

OUR GREATEST THREAT?
C-130, 463RD AIRLIFT GROUP, LITTLE ROCK AFB, ARK.

Name withheld by request, September 2008

Many of us have deployed to OIF and realised within a few flights that we face some unique challenges that may or may not have anything to do with aviating in combat. Some of these are dust storms that arise from nowhere, flash thunderstorms, heavy traffic, and airspace restrictions that make little sense to anyone but ATC. One consideration that most of us rarely have to deal with, outside of the AOR, is flying among UAVs, helps and various aircraft from the U.S., as well as Allied Nations. These differences take us even further out of our comfort zone and pose a unique and difficult challenge to everyone's overall safety. With this in mind, here's a situation that occurred on my last deployment.

My crew and I had just flown our C-130 on a typical 12-hour day, better known as the "pain train." We were tired, but still alert and on task. As usual, we had fought ATC for a while to get landing clearance between other aircraft departing and arriving, as well as the airfield attacks that are all too common. As the navigator, I was on the radios and gathered the paperwork from the crew. After landing, the tower allowed us to back taxi on one of the runways to get to our parking spot, a standard procedure due to some taxiway maintenance. About halfway down the runway, we heard the tower clear a fighter to land. We were on the runway that was the normal landing runway, but it was closed to departures and arrivals and used as a taxiway. The fighter got clearance to land on the other runway and seemed to be no factor.

The flight deck was relatively calm and quiet due to the checklists and radio calls winding down. We were about 100 yards from turning off of the runway and onto the taxiway to park, when I heard the co-pilot go out on the radio: "Aircraft on short final, aircraft on short final, GO-AROUND, GO-AROUND NOW!" I snapped my head up, jumped up to the window and tried to get a handle of what was going on. I saw a fighter aircraft pulling up hard to miss us. I'm not sure exactly how close the fighter aircraft was to us, but I do know that it was close enough that I could read some of the writing on the side of the aircraft. Our co-pilot declared that the aircraft was clear over the radio, and we continued to taxi.

Although we had just been amazingly lucky and we should've all been a bit nervous, the entire crew stayed on task and kept our heads. We parked, ran the engine shutdown checklist, and got ready to deplane. That's when the weight of what had just happened hit us like a ton of bricks. I realized how close my wife and kids were to collecting my SGLI.

Now, I have been under enemy fire, and I've had some scary things happen as a result of flying in combat, but I had really never felt as if I was actually in any form of imminent danger until now. I began to sweat and feel sick to my stomach, and then it quickly turned from fear and sickness to anger. The aircraft commander decided to file a HATR. The whole ops building was in an uproar about the incident, and the commander was already on the phone.

If it weren't for the co-pilot in our aircraft being on his game and having a good sense of situational awareness, up to seven lives could have been lost, two aircraft destroyed, and several missions delayed or cancelled because of it.

Lessons Learned:

1. Even after the day is just about done, one must stay alert and vigilant until the aircraft is in the chocks, the last checklist is complete, and the crew is safely inside their living quarters.
2. Although we were all flying in a combat environment and all task-saturated, we must never forget the basics and get complacent about where and how we fly. It's difficult to do, but we must stay vigilant. Just because you've gotten the same clearance every day for the last month, it could change at any time.
3. We can't let the idea of combat aviating and the adrenaline rush that follows haze our faculties and allow us to do silly things, like not looking outside of the aircraft and seeing a big plane with engines running in your landing path.

Sometimes it's better to be lucky than good, but you can't rely on luck. What we can rely on is our training and our ability to use the tools imparted to us by our trainers. Situational awareness is essential in increasing our day-to-day survivability as we risk our lives doing what we do.

Maintaining the standards set by our commanders and performing the tasks we practice is very important, especially when in combat with other distractions. Safety is paramount and should never be set aside. Our country, our careers and our lives depend on us watching out for each other and making the daily attempt to keep the entire operating environment safe for everyone. It's not just the right thing to do — it's the law.

NOTES:

FLIGHT DECK HABITS
C-17, OPERATIONAL INFORMATION WITHHELD

Name withheld by request, September 2008

One of the behavioral elements that makes an individual a good pilot is the ability to consistently complete a set of objectives. It's the ability to complete a set of checklist steps in the right order, the same way, every time, that makes a pilot successful. However, what happens when these habit patterns get interrupted? What happens when an aircraft emergency takes you out of your normal sequence in the aircraft? In these cases, your best behavioral ally can become your worst enemy.

After studying a variety of aircraft mishaps, an abrupt change in the normal sequence of events on a flight deck can cause even the most experienced pilot some difficulty. More experience in a particular aircraft could be a greater hazard when an unforeseen circumstance takes you out of the normal flow of events. The more times you complete a sequence of tasks, the more you expect and rely on that sequence to stay the same. You expect one task to lead you to the next, and the next until you have landed. However, when an event takes you out of your sequence, it may be difficult to remember to go back and accomplish the next step. That's why mishaps frequently occur out of abnormal, but benign circumstances. A C-17 sortie I experienced as a co-pilot is a great example of this potentially deadly behavior pattern.

As a co-pilot in the C-17 who became mission ready in the era following Sept. 11, 2001, I found myself thrust into combat situations early on in my career. In fact, my 4th flight in the C-17 was into Afghanistan. I was forced to learn quickly and adapt to the new flying environment of Southwest Asia. During one of my early trips into Afghanistan, I was with a relatively experienced crew. The IP had several thousand hours total time and was very experienced in the C-17. The co-pilot was one of their T-37 instructors during pilot training and was on their own C-17 aircraft commander upgrade mission. Therefore, I felt very comfortable watching and learning as this duo flew around in the AOR. On one particular mission, we were scheduled to fly from Camp Snoopy in Doha, Qatar to Kandahar, Afghanistan to resupply the base with a few pallets of food. Since we had already been flying in the Middle East for a few weeks, we learned nothing new during that day's intel/tactics briefing. There was always the threat of MANPADs and AAA fire anywhere in Afghanistan, and we were no strangers to these threats. We felt prepared to face any danger during our mission; however, it was the most innocuous threat that day which nearly led to disaster.

The flight from Qatar to Afghanistan was uneventful. It was only after we started our approach that we began to encounter trouble. It was customary to fly a steep spiral approach over the airfield to transition from the en route system to landing. The IP was the pilot flying and with the aircraft commander upgrade student not flying. I was sitting in one of the additional crew member seats to watch their procedures and back them up. As the IP began her steep spiral approach into the airfield, everything seemed to be going as briefed. Then, as we began our second and last circle over the field, we noticed a bright light a few miles from the field that appeared to be tracking our aircraft. We were being spotlighted. This is the event that distracted the crew and broke our normal sequence of events for landing.

Once the crew realized that we were being spotlighted, we all looked outside attempting to determine the exact location of the light so that we could brief Intel after we landed. However, as we were all looking outside, the aircraft was still descending at 4000-5000 feet per minute toward the ground on the approach. As a result of this distraction, the IP started to get behind the approach, and it became difficult to manage the descent rate and approach angle. The approach that had started out easy had become far more difficult. Eventually, we ended up on an angling final, well above a normal glide path, with the crew channelizing their attention on saving the approach.

Early on in Operation Enduring Freedom, it was an unspoken rule that you needed to land on your first approach. Your first approach allowed the enemy to know your location, and therefore, a second approach may expose the aircraft to targeting by enemy fire. There was significant pressure to put the aircraft on the ground the first time.

The pilot made every effort to recover from the errant approach, totally focused on that task alone. As a result, the IP recovered the aircraft to a normal landing approach by about 400 feet AGL. The crew then began to relax and continued with the approach. Suddenly, at 250 feet AGL, our Ground Proximity Warning System alerted us to a potential danger. "TOO LOW, GEAR," it shouted at us. As we all simultaneously realized that the gear was still up, the co-pilot slammed the gear handle down, and the pilot lessened the approach angle to allow enough time for the gear to be down and locked before touchdown. Shortly before touchdown, the gear was confirmed down. After completing the landing, we had some time to discuss what had just happened.

Our first mistake was allowing the entire crew to look outside at the spotlight to determine its location. None of us had been spotlighted before; otherwise, we would have realized this was a non-event. Our second mistake was allowing the spotlight to break our landing sequence of events, which eventually caused us to forget about completing the Before Landing Checklist. The checklist would have reminded us to put the gear down. Our last mistake was to not go-around early on before we got behind on the approach, or definitely when we realised that the gear wasn't down. Although the second approach may have exposed our crew to some additional threats, the biggest threat was damaging the aircraft by landing with the gear still in the well.

Lessons Learned:

As a result of this event, I added a step to my personal landing checks. I now verify the landing gear and our landing clearance at 1000 feet AGL. It's a step that I make every effort not to forget, even when things are going wrong. I brief my additional crew members that helping the crew to remember this step is their only job, even in an emergency situation. This last-chance safety check has made me a more confident and better pilot overall. I also make every effort to encourage my students to develop their own last-chance safety checks as well.

Even the most experienced pilots can be thrown out of their normal rhythms by random events. Therefore, when an unplanned event takes you out of your normal habit patterns, acknowledge the distraction or resolve the situation, then continue with your normal patterns — this will keep you from turning a bad situation into a potentially deadly one.

NOTES:

CHAPTER 7
HUMAN FACTORS

"**But failure is not a sign of weakness. It is a sign that you are alive and growing.**"

Colonel Buzz Aldrin, USAF

CROSS COUNTRY
F-15, OPERATIONAL INFORMATION WITHHELD

Name withheld by request, Nov 2008

There I was, in one of the best situations a flier can find himself/herself in, with the "keys" to a two-ship for the weekend. What could be better? This is the story of how the weekend turned into a leadership challenge, on the ground and in the air.

Several weeks before, as a flight commander, the director of operations told me I could take a two-ship anywhere I wanted, as long as the jets performed a fly-by for a race Saturday and returned Monday. I selected the other crew members and we began to plan for the weekend. We planned a simple one-sortie Friday, two-sortie Saturday, including the fly-by, and then a return to base Monday. However, because of many maintenance aborts, the squadron was behind on sorties, so the Thursday before, the DO told me we needed to come home Monday with at least eight sorties.

I scrambled all day coming up with a plan, dividing duties among the crews who were not flying and coordinating for PPRs, permission to land at a base and receive service. Our plan was to fly three sorties Friday — leave home station, fly a basic navigation flight to another military field, take off and fly a low-level to land at a training base to show the aircraft to students, and then a final sortie to land at a reserve/civilian field before dark. On Saturday — two air navigation flights to military fields to stage for the fly-by, and then the third sortie to perform the fly-by and land back where we started Saturday morning. On Monday — two basic sorties then return to our assigned base.

Friday began with completing the plan and getting underway. Only one issue arose as we finished our planning and went to base weather to coordinate. Significant weather was beginning to build throughout the southeast and could be an issue all weekend. However, all airfields were in the green and under VFR conditions. The first sortie was uneventful. We got a weather update saying that the weather should still support our plan. All the fields and diverts were in the green, but a look at the weather radar caused doubts to creep into my mind. As we began getting close to our next landing, a call to Metro told us the weather was now extremely bad and below our weather categories, and that our divert was under the same conditions. However, we got lucky and found a third base within range and with good weather. As we landed, I remembered thinking "That was a little more difficult than briefed," and I hoped the rest of the weekend would be better. The last flight of the day was uneventful, and we managed to arrive on time, only to learn that although we had a PPR, the crews who knew how to service our aircraft had departed for the day. Yet another omen of things to come. After another hour and a half of making calls and pleading, the crews returned and serviced the aircraft for the night. We got in our rooms within minutes of having crew rest for the schedule tomorrow.

Saturday began with weather barely above takeoff minimums and gusty winds, but within 10 minutes we were in clear air and had an enjoyable, relaxing first sortie. After eating and talking to weather, we took off again and enjoyed good conditions until 30 minutes before landing at the next location. Once again, we entered difficult conditions, although the weather was above minimums, and we broke out with several hundred feet to spare. As we landed and entered base ops, we began discussions with our ground crew and race officials about whether the fly-by would proceed. We ended up delaying on the ground for more than 30 minutes, waiting for word on whether to launch. Meanwhile, the same weather that built the day before was back and standing between us and getting to our final destination. However, because of the push to make the fly-by, we were unaware of the thunderstorms in our path. Finally, we learned that the fly-by had been cancelled, and we were cleared for takeoff, to fly straight to our final destination.

We took off and immediately entered the weather. Within 30 minutes, we got word of a large thunderstorm in front of the flight path. We coordinated with air traffic control for vectors around the system and to the final destination. As we moved around the initial cell, ATC informed us of more build-ups. Suddenly we were surrounded by thunderstorms, with all of our divert bases now in the red. We weighed our options and had several radio communications with military pilot to Metro stations. Finally, we decided our only option was to push through the final wall of storms and attempt to land at our planned base. We put our radars out front and began to dodge cell after cell inside the front. We lost radio contact with ATC several times before finally breaking through the cells and making the approach to our planned base. We broke out slightly above minimums and landed uneventfully. As we landed and began to talk, we realized how many lightning strikes we'd seen and just how lucky we'd been. After a day of relaxation, we flew our assigned sorties on Monday and RTB with no issues.

Lessons Learned:

We learned several lessons during that chaotic weekend.

As the mission changed from a basic three-sortie weekend to an eight-sortie marathon, aircrew members must ensure they get a very good feel for the weather forecast for that period. I recommend you look at radar yourself, do a face-to-face with the base forecaster, and ensure you have a good understanding of how your diverts and gas requirements could factor into the mission.

Don't allow ground crews and potential deadlines from fly-bys to change your step-time habits.

Don't get caught in situations where weather can build without your knowledge.

Overall, aircrew judgment and discipline are key factors that should not be left behind for sorties or fly-bys.

NOTES:

SPATIAL DISORIENTATION
F-16CJ, 35TH FIGHTER WING, MISAWA AB, JAPAN

Captain Travis Higbee, July 2008

There I was, descending from 4,000 to 2,000 feet above the ocean's surface in 30 degrees of left bank, turning from the 15 DME arc to final on the HI-ILS 28 penetration into Misawa AB, Japan. I was also letting the jet slow from 300 to 250 KIAS as I made the turn. This was my first instrument check in the F-16CJ since my FTU training at Kelly Air Force Base a year and a half ago. I hadn't flown a sortie before this one in two solid weeks, due to poor weather, but all my currencies were good, and I felt confident I could handle it.

The radio crackled.

"Fang 22 with chase, Misawa approach, you're cleared ILS approach 28 at Misawa. Call the final approach fix."

The thick Japanese-accented controller's voice was decently clear today. Some days they can be difficult to understand, but today I was in luck.

"Fang 22, cleared ILS 28, WILCO," I replied.

The weather was the typical Misawa rain clouds from 500 feet AGL to infinity, with an occasional broken deck of clear airspace. The clouds were especially dense today, and as I roamed around in them, I couldn't remember the last time I'd seen a visible horizon. My poor chase-ship was tucked in really close to prevent going "lost wingman," and he did his best to monitor my actions, which wasn't much because he had to fly so close to me. I was fully on the gauges, being smooth with control inputs to help out my wingman and praying I wouldn't do something stupid to hook my check ride. Suddenly, I realized my ears and my eyes weren't agreeing with each other on the spatial orientation of my aircraft. Left bank felt like level; up felt like down. My hand grew heavy as it tried to apply maneuvers my eyes were telling me were incorrect. In my mind's eye, with the ocean's surface growing quickly closer, the situation rapidly became very serious!

Somewhere back in my UPT days, an instructor once told me that you have three bags you carry with you every time you fly. Each one is filled with a different, yet essential item. The first bag is skill – your personal capacity, whether genetic or learned, to fly an aircraft (your stick and- rudder skills). The second is experience – all the whiles that time has taught you (that whole "something ain't right here" feeling). The third is plain old dumb luck (that "Wow, I'm glad that didn't happen!" thing). The idea behind these three bags is simple: put enough in your skill and experience bag that you'll never have to reach into your luck bag. You see, the luck bag is hard to keep full, and you never know when you'll find it empty. Thus the old adage, "A crash is when you run out of altitude, airspeed, good ideas and luck — all at the same time!" My IP's instructional words, given so many years before, must have etched themselves well enough onto my small 250 megabyte brain that my thoughts now turned to that little nugget of wisdom, as if to find a ray of sun on a cloudy day.

Flashback to training ... I'm no stranger to instrument flying. As FAIP at Vance, I spent hundreds of hours in the weather, many of them solo. I've felt the effects of spatial disorientation and have overcome it countless times. I've seen the effects of spatial disorientation on many students, and have instructed on its dangers, how to identify it, and how to overcome it. Notwithstanding this, I have one experience that dwarfs all my experiences with special disorientation.

When I was flying T-38As in UPT in November 2001, my instructor and I were taking off on my last T-38 ride of the course. It was an 87 ride that I needed to complete the required number of hours in the program. We were flying the departure on a round robin out of Vance Air Force Base, headed down to Oklahoma City to shoot an ILS or two before returning home. The weather was very cloudy and rainy with a few thunderstorms developing and dissipating throughout the area, which was standard for Oklahoma.

As we leveled off at 10,000 feet MSL between two decks of clouds that completely obscured the sky and the ground, but left us in a small layer of clear airspace, I realized I'd completely lost track of which way was up. I felt like I was upside down! The eyes and ears were in total disagreement. I fought to keep the jet upright. My hands instinctively wanted to roll the jet over without my consent. It took every ounce of concentration I had to not do what my gauges said could kill me – roll inverted. The Giant Hand syndrome set in. I trimmed the best I could and then loosened my round grip on the stick. With my hand an inch away from the controls, I physically couldn't roll the jet over. I said to my instructor over the intercom, "I'm really spatially D'd right now; it feels like I'm upside down. I think you should take the jet." The response was less than reassuring. "I'm not any better than you are!" I later found out in the debrief that sitting in the back seat had spatially disoriented my instructor worse than me. Great, now it was up to me. I had to fight through it. Training rushed to mind. Fly the plane first! I ignored every radio call made over the next 15-30 seconds. Luckily, none were for us. I stared at the attitude indicator like it was the prettiest supermodel I had ever seen. To keep from losing altitude, I had to keep my pitch neutral. I had to kill any VVI. I set the power to a known RPM to keep the airspeed constant. I had to keep those stubby wings upright! I had to keep everything constant and wait. Wait for the brain to re-cage itself. Miraculously, at the time, it worked. Suddenly, my mind flipped everything right side up again, and I was on my merry way, as if nothing had happened. But something had happened. I had added a vital piece of wisdom to my bag of experience.

Back to today ... I swooped down over the Pacific Ocean in one of the world's premier spatial-disorientation machines (the F-16), turning, decelerating, configuring, checking radar, talking on radios, and doing it all in the weather at 2,000 feet above the absolute floor. I realized I was completely disoriented. Up felt like down, and left felt like level. Today, however, I didn't have to reach into my bag of luck. Instead, I reached into my bag of experience and pulled out the ray of light on a cloudy day.

When faced with seemingly incapacitating spatial disorientation, get the nose up to the horizon (which felt like I was pulling down toward the ocean's surface) and keep airspeed and altitude constant, then sit and stare at the attitude indicator and let the mind figure it out. I pulled back on the stick and added power to keep the airspeed constant. I pinned the attitude indicator center dot above the horizon and crosschecked that my VVI was zero and my airspeed was steady. I then began the nerve-wracking task of waiting.

Seconds seem like eternity. The Heavy Hand syndrome was so strong that I was unable to get the jet out of 30 degrees of bank, but that didn't matter. I had lots of room to turn over the Pacific Ocean, but not a lot of altitude to lose. I turned at 20-30 degrees, but the airspeed and the altitude stayed constant. About 20 seconds later, my mind re-caged. I made a turn back to final without incident. I had eluded disaster.

Thoughtfully pondering what my instructor had told me so long ago, I gratefully placed yet another piece of wisdom into my bag of experience.

NOTES:

GOT THE "ITIS"?

C-130, 39TH AIRLIFT SQUADRON, DYESS AFB, TEXAS

Captain Bryon T. Shields, Summer 2012

After four years of deploying overseas as a C-130H navigator, I finally landed the coveted "Iron-Swap" mission. The mission was to deliver a freshly refurbished C-130 from Dyess Air Force Base, Texas, to the Middle East to replace another C-130 due to its required maintenance inspections. Since our departure for the 10-day trip was scheduled for Dec. 9, we knew we might miss Christmas with our families. However, we had 16 days before Christmas and figured that was plenty of time to complete the 16,000-mile mission.

The mission went well until we picked up the aircraft that had been flying in the bone-dry climates of the Middle East and took it to the cold, wet climate that was typical of Mildenhall Air Base, England, in mid- December. There we encountered our first maintenance delays due to electrical problems with the generator control units. We ended up stepping to fly four out of five days and took off once only to return to Mildenhall when the No. 4 prop spinner gushed hydraulic fluid over Scotland. We eventually left Mildenhall with a new prop, but we were down a generator.

We landed in Prestwick, Scotland, to top off our tanks and then took off over the North Atlantic into an 80-knot headwind for a seven-hour trip to St. John's, Newfoundland, Canada. After a long flight of overwater procedures and listening to the scratchy high frequency radio, I was relieved to see the coast slowly brighten up my radar scope. The day went smoothly until we were on a seven-mile final for the straight-in visual to the runway. The pilot called for "gear down," then the co-pilot promptly responded with "Gear down," and he lowered the gear handle. However, the cranky, cold 50-year-old Herk responded by lowering only the nose gear. We knew it wasn't good because we only had about an hour of extra gas to resolve the problem. We were about three miles out and 900 feet above ground level. We went around, and notified the tower of our intentions to miss the approach and hold on the published holding point to troubleshoot the problem. Meanwhile, we discussed the Dash 1 procedure. About two minutes after the gear handle was lowered, the left main came down and then we felt the rights release and lower. The indicator showed all the gear down and locked, and the loadmaster confirmed by looking through the small wheel well windows. We entered the downwind and landed uneventfully.

We all knew our flying crew chiefs were going to say that there was nothing they could do there – zero maintenance support or jacks to lift the aircraft for a gear inspection. We had only a couple of days to get back to Dyess Air Force Base before the Christmas weekend. I told the pilots it would take 16 hours of flight time to get to Texas while flying with gear down and straight headwind of around 80 knots. The aircraft commander worked with the higher-ups to get a one-time gear down waiver and duty day extension from 16 to 18 hours.

We showed the next day after 14 hours on the ground for the last legs of our trip. At this point, we just wanted to get home. You could say we had the "itis" – the "get-home-itis." We were limited to a maximum indicated airspeed of 165 knots with the gear down, and scheduled to land at Westover ARB, Mass., for customs and gas.

Flying at 160 gave us a true airspeed of more than 200, however, a lovely headwind of 60 to 80 knots meant our groundspeed wasn't good. After a six-hour flight to Westover ARB, we quick-turned through customs, gas and flight planning for the final leg.

The winds were right on the limit of making it to Dyess at the end of our 18-hour duty day. We decided to press on and hope for the best. After going around some winter weather, we noticed we weren't looking good on time, and starting looking at Little Rock Air Force Base, La., as a possible alternate. I told the pilots we had to descend if we were to make it to Texas in time. We tried it, and the gamble paid off. The winds were significantly better at 12,000 feet versus 18,000 feet. We shut down the engines on the exact minute of our 18-hour limit. We took a risk knowing we would be close, and we were fortunate we didn't encounter more maintenance or weather issues.

Lessons Learned:

We were glad to finally be done, but we all agreed that we wouldn't do that again. We'd left ourselves with zero time for the "what-if's" like missing an approach and proceeding to an alternate. We backed ourselves into a corner and came close to breaking our duty-day limit and our own personal fatigue limit, as well.

The point is: Don't lean so far forward that you end up falling on your face. The mission is to get home to your families every time, not by a certain time. Important dates and family will wait for you.

Just be careful not to fall victim to the "itis".

NOTES:

AIR REFUELLING HAZARD
B-1B BOMBER, 560 FTS/DOC, RANDOLPH AFB, TX

Captain Sig Jucknies, April 2008

It was my 14th sortie in the AOR, and I was pretty comfortable with the routine. The sortie began like any other: standard brief, a stop at life support, and a short bread truck ride to our home for the next 16 hours. No incident was going to prevent me from completing my preflight and launching this combat mission. The takeoff and five-hour flight to the AOR were uneventful.

The sortie started off fairly active for a late-evening flight. We started the vul, fulfilling the assigned air support requests, and soon responded to multiple troops-in-contact situations. About nine hours into our sortie, we contacted our scheduled tanker and coordinated to move the air refueling point over the troops in contact that we were supporting. After blocking the airspace we needed with ATC, the rendezvous went as advertised, and we were established in the precontact position several minutes later.

The air was fairly turbulent over the refueling point, undoubtedly because of the high mountains under the new location. This was not much of a factor, since both pilots were very proficient, getting to air refuel at least four times per combat sortie. This night presented us with another challenge, though. The boom light on the KC-135 that illuminates the green and red bands on the boom was inoperative, making it very difficult to see the closure trends during refueling. In a B-1, the refueling receptacle is a few feet in front of the windscreen, making the boom one of our primary references.

We asked the tanker crew to turn on their flood light to help illuminate the boom, and that helped a little bit. We could make out the markings on the boom that defined the envelope, but couldn't see them clearly. We talked about the lack of detail that we could see from the front cockpit, but decided to continue and refuel, keeping in mind the troops below who were taking enemy fire. We connected with the tanker and began onloading fuel. We were scheduled for an onload of 65,000 pounds.

After taking on about 15,000 pounds of fuel, the air became a little more turbulent, making it more difficult to stay stable in the contact position. During the day that would have been a moderately simple task, but at night with poor visual cues, it was a bit more of a challenge. At one point, I started falling aft in the envelope and pushed up the throttles to move back into the heart of the envelope. Before too long, I found myself beginning a pilot-induced oscillation. We started moving forward and aft in the envelope, getting closer to the edges where it would be necessary to disconnect.

It wasn't long before I decided to disconnect and move back to the precontact position and attempt a more stabilized refueling. I was at the front of the envelope, very close to the forward limit of the boom, and cracked the throttles in order to start an aft trend. Soon after this, I pressed the boom-disconnect button on our jet. Normally, that would release the boom and cause a disconnect generated by our aircraft. On that occasion, nothing happened. I pressed the button again, as we were quickly moving to the aft limits of the boom. Again, the action was not successful. The other pilot in my jet pressed the disconnect button on his stick with no success, either. At that point we were at the aft limit, but the jet was not disconnecting from the boom. This caused the KC-135 and the B-1 to start a trend back toward each other in the vertical direction. I had seen enough and simultaneously pulled the throttles to almost an idle position and pushed forward on the stick, causing a brute force disconnect between the two aircraft. The disconnect was harsh and led to a breakaway call from the boom operator. We were already descending well below the tanker's altitude.

After the breakaway, we could hear an increase in wind noise over our air refueling receptacle. We decided not to close the receptacle door until we could get the boom operator to inspect the area. We moved back into the precontact position and asked the boom operator to take a look. She used the boom receptacle light to illuminate the B-1's receptacle. All she could see was some bent metal, but couldn't tell if the damage would prevent further refueling. She told us that she, too, had tried several times to initiate a disconnect, without success. After consulting with the crew, we decided to terminate air refueling. We raised our bingo fuel to our divert base by 10,000 pounds to account for any extra drag on the aircraft, and continued to support the TIC. We notified the ground troops that we only had 1.5 hours of play time remaining before we had to return to base. During the rest of our vul, we coordinated with the CAOC and other applicable agencies for an early departure from the AOR to our divert base. We closely monitored our fuel to ensure that we had no fuel leaking from our aircraft. The RTB was uneventful.

After landing, we discovered that the air refueling receptacle had torn out of the B-1, but we didn't know the reason for the disconnect failure. Less than a week later, this same incident happened again with a different KC-135 and B-1, highlighting that this was not an isolated incident. Inspections were done of the B-1s and the KC-135s, and we developed some interim procedures to prevent further incidents in the AOR. No further incidents occurred during the deployment.

Lessons Learned:

During training, having the boom light being out at night would have sent us home, but to support the troops on the ground, it was important that we refuel and get back in the fight.

Given this situation again, I would make the same decision to air refuel, but would probably move the track away from the mountains to avoid the further complications generated by turbulence.

During combat operations, we as pilots, sometimes have to take more risks than we would during peacetime operations. If risks cannot be mitigated, and the importance of the mission warrants continuing, a plan should be devised to prevent multiple risks from compounding into a disastrous situation.

NOTES:

FISHING BOAT IN THE SKY
F-16, 944TH FIGHTER WING, LUKE AFB, ARIZ.

Major Tim Stretch, September 2008

Have you ever seen Gary Larson's "The Far Side" cartoon in which two pilots are wondering what a mountain goat is doing "way up" in the clouds? That cartoon used to make me laugh — until a similar event happened to me!

I was part of an F-16 three-ship on a typical Air Combat Maneuvering training mission. My role as No. 3 was "bandit," to fly as a single Red Air adversary against the two other Blue Air fighters.

We briefed the sortie and knew that the weather would be a factor. When our flight entered the overwater airspace, we encountered a solid cloud deck about 2,000 feet above the water. There also was a solid overcast ceiling at about 15,000 feet. In between these two cloud decks, the area was clear and the visibility was unlimited. I could actually see a horizon in all directions. Flight lead confirmed we'd use the briefed fight floor of 5,000 feet. We accomplished a "G-check" to test proper operation of the G-suit inflation and positive pressure breathing equipment. The G-check was also a chance to practice my L-1 straining maneuver, and served as a reminder that I was about to enter a dangerously high G environment. My adrenalin was flowing, and I felt eager to hear those two words: "Fight's On!"

After four dynamic, high-speed, high-G ACM engagements, I determined I had enough gas for just one more setup. I built some range and airspeed for the final engagement. As I accelerated to 500 KIAs and gained approximately 10nm of separation from the fighters, I had a brilliant idea ... I would perform an Immelman back into the fighters, thus changing altitude from low to high, and hopefully gain an advantage for the last merge. What I did next put me right into a Class E spacial disorientation event.

My Immelman was performed at over 9 Gs. I didn't stay on top of my G-strain, and as the blood rushed out of my brain, my vision suffered, and everything started going white. So I hunkered down on my G-strain, which forced the blood back into my brain, and I regained my vision. I pulled to the horizon and finished what I thought was my Immelman. What I didn't know was that while visually impaired, I had actually over-pulled and nearly performed a loop. This is when the spatial D set in: I thought I had executed an Immelmann which ends with a roll upright — my roll to "upright" actually rolled me inverted.

Something didn't feel right (because I was upside down). But because I was descending, the jet was still under 1 G, so I was experiencing the normal upright 1 G feeling, although I was inverted. My brain was telling me I was right side up, because I never recognized the pull through the Immelman into a loop. Since it didn't feel right, I instinctively tried to confirm my attitude and recover. Looking outside, I could see the horizon. The problem was, I couldn't tell which way was up due to the cloud layers both above and below me. I transitioned to instruments inside the cockpit to confirm my attitude. My main ADI indicated I was inverted. I felt that couldn't possibly be correct because my brain was still telling me that I had performed an Immelman and was right side up.

I looked at my standby attitude indicator, but it had tumbled during my manoeuvring and was useless. I made a slow aileron roll from inverted, to right side up, to inverted again, trying to determine my attitude. I checked my altitude and noticed I was still above the floor, but I didn't understand why I was descending when I felt I should be climbing. I was so spatially disoriented, I thought about ejection if I couldn't quickly figure something out. Then, while still flying inverted, a small fishing boat (Gary Larson's mountain goat) appeared briefly through the clouds. For a split second, I thought "What the heck is a boat doing way up here in the clouds?" It was then that I recognized my spatial D, rolled upright, and recovered.

I "knocked it off" and returned to base. After landing, I told my squadron leadership about the event. There would be some valuable lessons learned. Lucky for me, I got to personally brief those lessons at the next wing safety meeting.

Lessons Learned:

My three main points (SOS grad) pertained to training rules, anti G-strain, and recovery from unusual attitudes. First, I unknowingly broke an ACBT training rule in 11-214. It states that among other weather requirements, you must have a "discernible horizon." I never really thought about what "discernible" meant until this event. You need to know which way is up and which way is down. Sounds pretty basic, but it took a disorienting event to make me understand the importance of that training rule.

Second, my G-strain was not sufficient for the maneuver I performed. I never had problems with Gs in the past, but no matter how experienced you are, G-onset can be fast and fatal if you aren't ready. This event occurred on our fifth ACM engagement; I was getting tired and my G-tolerance was weakened. Also, I was complacent and didn't perform my G-strain correctly. I reviewed my tapes with a flight surgeon, and it became clear to me that my breathing technique went from textbook during the first few sets to poor on that last set. Instead of easing off of the Gs, I simply elected to strain harder while maintaining maximum G. Bad move. I should've eased off like I was taught to do in centrifuge training. It's imperative to recognise that our ability to sustain Gs can seriously degrade with fatigue, especially during missions like BFM and ACM. For me, a 9 G Immelman was not a smart tactic on my fifth ACM set. Know your limits and fly the jet accordingly.

Third, while spatially disoriented, I trusted the "seat of my pants" sensations instead of the instruments. My brain was telling me I was upright due to the expected maneuver, but my main ADI indicated (correctly) my inverted attitude. The brain can be a very powerful liar and has caused numerous physiological mishaps. It takes an enormous amount of fortitude to crosscheck all of your instruments, analyze the situation, and recover the aircraft based on logic instead of feel. You can't just blindly trust your instruments (as evident from my standby ADI), but if looking outside doesn't help, realize that your brain may try and dissuade you from trusting a perfectly functioning ADI.

As a final note, if you ever experience spatial disorientation, remember to tell your safety representative. If it could happen to you, it could happen to anyone else. We can all learn from others' experiences. Hopefully you can learn from my encounter on the Far Side and won't have to rely on mountain goats or fishing boats to determine which way is up.

NOTES:

RISK VS THREAT
OPERATIONAL INFORMATION WITHHELD

Name withheld by request, Oct 2008

The following article deals with the challenge of balancing risk within a high threat environment. How much risk are we willing to accept to achieve the desired outcome, and what are the consequences of accepting the additional risk?

The following scenario is a good example of accepting too much risk to avoid one threat, while simultaneously exposing the aircraft to an additional threat.

I was a new aircraft commander on one of my first rides in theater. The weather was clear and free from clouds and this was our first stop of the night. En route to our stop, we discussed look out doctrine and who was going to scan for threats and where, as well as how we were going to run the required briefings and checklists. We also talked about how we were going to set up our aircraft lighting. We had a brief from squadron tactics on the midair threat and how some crews were having close calls with other aircraft, particularly helicopters, as well as our normal enemy threat briefings. I chose to focus more on the enemy threat since I assumed most aircraft in the terminal area would be under radar or tower control, so our midair threat should be reduced. After the long flight en route, we were finally ready to start our descent from altitude.

We were on a visual approach into an airfield in theater with normal NVG lighting. After commencing the approach, I heard a formation of helicopters asking for permission to depart to the east. Nothing seemed out of the ordinary, and I expected the departure course to be well clear of my approach. We received permission to land, so I assumed tower would be providing adequate approach separation. On an approximate two-mile final, I observed the formation of two helicopters, also blacked out, fly in front of my aircraft over the threshold lights. Although both of our aircraft were blacked out, I visually acquired them with my NVGs. Since they were directly in front of me, it was fairly easy to acquire them; however, we were at a 90-degree angle to them, so unless they were looking, they probably didn't see our aircraft. At this point, we were busy running checklists and preparing for landing, scanning outside the aircraft, and ensuring we completed required checklists. Inside the one-mile point, I noticed another pair of blacked-out helicopters transition across my flight path over the threshold lights right in front of my aircraft. I immediately initiated a climb due to the proximity of the helicopters to my flight path. After they passed by and were no longer a threat to the aircraft, I continued the approach and landed safely. If I hadn't seen the additional two helicopters and continued on the descent profile, we would've been dangerously close to a midair collision.

Flying in theater requires balancing risk mitigation between the two most significant threats: enemy fire and midair collision with coalition aircraft. One of the first briefings we get when we arrive in theatre is balancing the two threats. On one extreme, we can deny the enemy acquiring our aircraft at night by blacking out the aircraft to such an extent that we will be virtually unseen. This decreases the enemy acquisition threat, but conversely exposes the aircraft to a midair threat. On the other extreme, we can fly with our normal aircraft lighting to enable see-and-avoid with other aircraft flying in the area. This would minimize the likelihood of a midair collision, but would expose aircrew unnecessarily to visual acquisition by the enemy and, subsequently, enemy ground fire.

Another way to look at the problem is to use a sliding scale. On one side, for example, you have the enemy threat. On the other side you have the midair threat. Theoretically, we should fly somewhat in the middle, balancing both threats, accepting some risk from one threat while negating risk from the other threat. If you move too much to one extreme, you may mitigate most of a threat, but now you have overly exposed yourself to the other threat that could be equally as deadly.

For me, I perceived the most significant threat to be enemy fire. Due to the perceived threat, I elected to fly the approach as blacked out as possible. As we can see from the above scenario, I was closer to the enemy risk avoidance on the risk scale, while not paying enough attention to the midair threat, and by flying to mitigate that threat, overly exposed myself to a possible air traffic conflict with friendly helicopters.

In subsequent flights, I elected to fly the approach blacked out and then turn on some overt lighting closer into the airfield to aid in visual acquisition for other aircraft. This approach seemed to be the best balance for the level of risk at the terminal phase of flight in preparation of landing. I also understated the role that the airfield tower played in the above situation. Although not as tactically sound, I could've given the tower my relative position to the airfield to enable other aircraft to have a greater situational awareness as to my aircraft's position relative to their position. Given this, the helicopters might have held their position and waited for us to land before dragging their formation in front of us, or tower could have directed them to hold, thus eliminating the possible midair.

Lessons Learned:

In a chaotic environment of numerous aircraft transiting the terminal environment, as well as an enemy trying to shoot down coalition aircraft, we need to decide which is the appropriate risk mitigation technique we're going to use and when on the descent profile we're going to use them.

Also, don't underestimate the power of basic communication between aircraft and the controlling services. If tower has more information, they can easily break a chain in a potential mishap situation. Everyone has a role in the ORM process, outside and inside of the aircraft.

NOTES:

PUSHING JUST TO CHECK A BOX
MC-130H COMBAT TALON II, OPERATIONAL INFORMATION WITHHELD

Name withheld by request, Oct 2008

It was a dark and gloomy night in Alaska, barely VFR.

Our MC-130H "Combat Talon II" rumbled through the night on a low-level TF training sortie. As part of our training profile, we terminated our regular radar TF procedures and started to perform NVG low-level. The difference is that when using radar TF procedures, the radar is looking out approximately 20 NM to generate a flying profile from 250 to 1,000 feet, regardless of the visibility.

Using NVG low-level procedures, we dim down our displays or turn off the radar TF generated profile and fly a visual modified contour profile, with only the radar altimeter to give us any low altitude warning protection down to 300 feet. After 30 +/- minutes from Elmendorf at the end of a 4.5 sortie, flying NVG low-level, the low-alt warning went off; bells and whistles pierced the cockpit. I pulled hard on the yoke and applied full power; the RADALT maintained 115 to 150 feet as the Talon II clawed its way up the mountainside. The crew breathed a collective sigh of relief as we crested the ridge. We activated the TF system and followed the valley home. The flight deck was silent as the crew contemplated how close to death we really were, and for what?

A highly trained, seasoned and irreplaceable crew was almost killed that night because we were pushing the weather to check a box! In the marginal VFR, almost zero illumination night, we failed to see a ridge jutting off the side of the valley we were in. We train to fly not down the middle of valleys, but on one side or the other — illumination, winds and threat dependant. Due to the low illumination, the ridge was basically invisible.

Luckily the day before, on a severe clear VFR TF training line, the IP I was flying with stressed the necessity to respond aggressively to all low altitude warnings and not grow complacent to the systems designed to protect you. Sometimes, when not utilizing the radar TF mode, a small finger ridge or a very tall tree will give you a brief low altitude warning, but often you're past the object by the time you react.

It's important to verbalize an impending low altitude warning to let the rest of the crew know you've identified the object which is driving the warning. You can lull yourself into thinking that when the warning goes off, it must be for something you've identified. That's where you can lead yourself into a false sense of security because you're second-guessing a protective system. The conditions were ripe that night for a CFIT event, but luckily, we reacted correctly and can now tell the tale.

Although the Talon II is an advanced aircraft with unrivaled all-weather TF capability, all that technology can make you think you're invincible due to the comprehensive safeguard systems that are in place. Many other aircraft perform low-level ops utilizing far less sophisticated equipment, but the same ideas apply to all aviators that fly within hundreds of feet off the ground, often in poor weather, and now more often in hostile territory. The bottom line is that we have to be on top of our game all the time, regardless if we're flying an F-22, MC-130H or a Cessna 182. We have to thoroughly understand our equipment and, more importantly, our equipment's limitations.

Usually we work hard to keep our semiannual requirements under control, but the next time you're pushing to fill a square, think twice. The worst that can happen is that you have to fly with an instructor for the first ride of the next semiannual. Big deal, better than being a smoking hole! I have heard good commanders and DOs stress the importance of safety, and stress that if you're asked to do something unsafe, there'll be a good reason for it, usually coming from the highest AF and DoD levels. Usually the stress we feel to check a box doesn't come from the head office, but from ourselves or our peers. Aviation in general is a culture of competition, striving for success with a work hard/play hard attitude. All these traits are good for a powerful and victorious Air Force, but like Clint Eastwood says, "Every man has to know his limitations." I support the idea of max-performing the aircraft, getting the most out of each training line, as long as we temper this with a culture that will accept aviators "knocking it off" to live and train/ fight another day.

Lessons Learned:

The more we razz each other about making conservative decisions or talk about how someone is a wimp because they didn't push it to get requirements done, the more likely we'll set someone up to push themselves and their crews past their limits and into death's door. The mishap report annals are full of good crews that pushed themselves too hard and died on vanilla training lines ... and for what? Like anything in life, a common ground is important.

Our jobs as aviators are inherently dangerous. We should savor our abilities to get a mission accomplished, train ourselves to the edge to ensure we're the most lethal Air Force in the world, but be aware of our personal and equipment limits.

NOTES:

CLOSE CALL AFTER SUNSET
F-15C, 95TH FIGHTER SQUADRON, TYNDALL AFB, FLA.

Captain Brad "Mute" Ertmer, Oct 2008

At the time, I was a 150-hour invincible wingman ready to take on the world. What I saw not only changed my attitude, but also changed how I brief, execute and debrief every night sortie I fly. Hopefully, this will give you a different perspective and a newfound respect for the machines we have the privilege of flying.

It was the third week of a one-month deployment flying Dissimilar Air Combat Training in F-15Cs as red air against F-16s gaining blue training. This was the first week of night sorties after two weeks of day flying. My flight of six arrived to what by now was a fairly standard brief with the only addition being night and night vision goggle specifics. Following the coordination brief, my flight lead briefed up our red air (simulating MiG 29 Fulcrums) game = plan and night deconfliction plan. About half an hour after sunset, I suited up and stepped to my jet for what I thought would be an uneventful sortie, followed by late evening cocktails downtown. This evening was anything but uneventful.

As the blue air flight lead called "Fight's on," I pressed out of my

CAP in my block (a sanctuary altitude that cannot be transited unless a very specific set of criteria exist – especially at night). After five minutes, the blue air F-16s and my flight of F-15s met at the merge. Feeling good about being undetected by the blue air, I saw a two-ship of F-16s in the beam off my nose above me at about 22,000 feet MSL (the F-16 blocks were the 0-4s – i.e., 10,000-14,000 feet; 20,000-24,000 feet, etc.) with my NVGs. Regardless of range or aspect angle, other jets on NVGs appear as a spot of light, so other means such as radar or GCI must be used to determine actual slant range distance to what the eyeball is seeing. At first, the two-ship had distinct line of sight across my canopy bow (they weren't pointed at me). Suddenly, the line of sight froze on my canopy bow, meaning that the F-16s had either turned directly away from me or had turned nose on to get a radar lock and shoot. It turns out to be the latter.

A second later, I received a radar spike on my radar warning receiver. In debrief, I learned the range the two-ship turned into me was approximately four miles. At mach vs. mach speeds, this equates to about 12 seconds until we're in the same exact piece of sky, if neither of us flinch. I wasn't worried yet as I was in my block at 18,000 feet and expecting the F-16s to stay in their block at >20,000 feet MSL. I should have been worried as the lead F-16 determined he had fulfilled all requirements to come out of his block and into mine with his nose pointed straight at me. After seeing his flight lead turn hard to the left and descend, the trail F-16 followed his flight lead without ever seeing the threat (me) that was four NM away and closing. From here on, time dilation began to kick in as I watched the pinpoint of light that was a jet blossom into the fully recognisable form of the lead F-16 as he passed 500 feet off my left wing. If everything is done correctly IAW 11-214 training rules, there's no way I should have seen anything more than a spot of light, and the F-16 shouldn't have been closer than 1,000 feet away. This was enough for me to know that I had enough, but the best was yet to come.

The trail F-16 was one NM back from his flight lead and still didn't see me. One NM of range equates to three seconds of time.

This three seconds lasted forever in my mind as again I saw an F-16 erupt from a pinpoint of light to an F-16 which I not only could VID, but could identify the other pilot's helmet – at night, at 1,200+ knots of closure, and, as it turns out, 199 feet away from me. My brain took several seconds to register what had just happened as I started a shallow turn to the left to get away as soon as possible. Following a plethora of choice four-letter words, I removed my tactical flying mindset and shifted immediately to self-preservation and got as far from the other jets as possible (>50 NM) and waited until the end of the fight to RTB. Needless to say, the debrief was slightly tense as a midair collision had nearly occurred. Only the lead F-16 had seen me – the trail F-16 (the 199 feet pass F-16) had not seen me nor knew I was there even after the close pass.

Lessons Learned:

Two major lessons can be gleaned from what was nearly a tragic incident with loss of two lives and millions of dollars of Air Force combat assets. The first regarded the NVG crosscheck negative transfer from day to night, and the second more important lesson was adherence to training rules, which are written in blood and were very nearly rewritten in blood.

Negative transfer is defined as taking a habit pattern that works during one set of circumstances and transposing it to a similar, though not identical, set of circumstances, resulting in an adverse effect. As it relates to this situation, the transfer occurred due to a visual cue that during the day would dictate one set of actions. When a pilot sees an enemy jet in the daylight, his first instinct is to employ ordnance by ripping his nose directly to the bandit while "bore sighting" with the radar – putting what you see right on the nose to get a radar lock. Under these conditions, a pilot has two essential pieces of data directly from his eye – depth perception and shape of the jet.

Instantly, the subconscious processes the data to the invaluable pieces of required information – range as deduced from depth perception and aspect angle as deduced by the shape of the jet and line-of-sight direction. If the other jet is too close, the pilot simply stops pulling his nose on before pointing directly at the bandit so as not to cause a collision.

Now take that set of circumstances and change the illumination to night and add NVGs. As described earlier, a jet on NVGs looks like a spot of light until well inside of 1,000 feet. A spot of light gives no data about depth perception or aspect angle – the two essential data needed to make an instantaneous determination about collision avoidance. A pilot inexperienced with NVGs (or extremely task-loaded) will revert to trusting his primary sensory input – his eyeball. The pilot must recognize that his eyeball is not giving him all the information it gives during the day and fight the tendency to point at the bandit. In my case, the pilot did exactly what he would do during the day, and the results speak for themselves.

The second lesson learned from this case is a reiteration of the necessity to obey training rules. It's precisely at the merge that training rules are most important. In this case, the lead F-16 pilot had a spot of light that he used as justification to exit his block and enter mine. In order to exit the block on a visual commit at night, one must have range awareness, a visible line of sight and a visible horizon. The spot of light that was my jet led the pilot to believe he had range awareness. Also, the required line of sight wasn't present. The only criterion fulfilled on this event was a visible horizon. The trail fighter had even less reason to leave his block as he didn't have situational awareness on my jet even being there. At night, your assigned block is where you MUST be, unless, beyond a shadow of a doubt, you have spatial awareness of every jet involved – a near impossible feat. This training rule point MUST be emphasized in the brief. The other point that I now emphasize during my briefs, while not necessarily a training rule violation, is that bore sight radar modes are the last choice of modes to use at night – off axis, slewable modes are primary visual auto acquisition modes at night.

Looking back on what happened that night, I'm not sorry it occurred, and I don't blame the other pilot. Before this event, given the same set of circumstances, with the roles reversed, I may have done exactly as the F-16 pilot had done with the exact same results. Each of these "pucker factor" sorties helps to teach us an invaluable set of lessons for the future. My hope is that those of you reading this can painlessly learn a lesson from me without such a close call.

NOTES:

GO GREEN OR GO HOME
C-17, 437 AIRLIFT WING, CHARLESTON AFB, SC

Captain Jason Hughes, April 2008

It was probably the 20th sortie of the month, and by this time, my crew and I had grown accustomed to this type mission: go from "Base One" to "Base Two" to upload cargo, and then on to "Base Three" for delivery. Nothing about this load was different from any other, and the flight duty period was the average 16-hour day. It was, however, extremely hot, and due to the very high weight of the load, we had some problems carrying enough fuel to make it all the way back home at the end of the day. We knew fueling downrange was a must, and we tankered as much gas as we could. The heat was a difficult obstacle. After all the fueling and loading was complete, we crunched our numbers and were set to go. It was going to be a long T/O run and a slow climb to altitude! Everything went fine, and we were soon at cruise and on our way. We studied the weather en route and called for an update about an hour out, which was clear skies and a little windy on the ground — nothing that should raise eyebrows.

"Base Three" is a location I had flown to several times, as well as having flown in and out of other nearby bases multiple times. After studying the terrain chart and arrival I wanted, I briefed the crew on what to expect on approach and what we should see. It was dark, and "Base Three" was definitely in mountainous terrain. I talked to the other pilots, and we agreed that because the field lay in the middle of the city, washout would be very bad, and because we would be clear of the mountains before our descent, we weren't going to wear our night vision goggles. I wasn't a fan of them anyway, and many of the fields now have serious washout problems, and coordination is usually a hassle, causing more trouble than anything. About 30 minutes out, we started to see the city where the airfield lies and the mountains around them. Before we knew it, we completed our checklists and were getting clearance to descend and begin our approach. I pulled the throttles, started down and WOW! Huge mountains were just below our flight path, and they sure seemed close. According to the chart, our current altitude and descent rate, we should have been fine. I thought to myself, "It sure would be nice to have those NVGs now!" We continued and cleared the mountains fine, as I felt the release of tension I had built up coming over them in the dark. All this time, my co-pilot was on the radio getting nowhere with the controller, who evidently thought we were going somewhere else.

After extended vectors and many frequency changes, we got in touch with the correct tower controller and were told to continue on approach, but that there was a vehicle on the runway, and the controller wasn't sure if it was gone yet. Around 1,500 feet AGL, we were configured and were approaching short final with no landing clearance, as the tower radioed, asking us to make a 360 degree turn, present position, because he still wasn't sure about the vehicle on the runway. This was starting to feel very much like one of those stories you read about. We turned around, and by the time we rolled out again, tower had given us clearance to land. While in the turn and directly over the city we most wanted to avoid, I thought, "I'm sure glad I didn't wear those NVGs, because I would have been blinded." As we came through 1,000 feet, my co-pilot told me the winds were very high, almost at our limit by a couple knots on the nose and from the left. I definitely felt them as I fought to keep the wing down and applied enough force on the rudder. I told him to watch the winds and to send me around if they got any worse. I was thankful they didn't, and we made a very lively touchdown, for lack of a better description. As we taxied clear and parked, I realized my hands were shaking, and my legs were stiff. The other pilots applauded and were thankful to be on the ground after that ride. The whole time I was thinking to myself, "That was really stupid; those mountains could have come up and bit us, and we would have never seen them." At that moment, I made the decision to depart on NVGs, regardless of the city lights. I'm not going to take another chance with those mountains again. We discussed the departure plan and agreed that we will wear the NVGs until we reach an altitude above the mountains.

Once we finished the download and got fuel, we cranked engines, and I put on my helmet and NVGs so that I could taxi, while my co-pilot briefed the departure one last time and readied himself to fly. What I didn't notice was that he was still wearing his headset, no NVGs, and we were now sitting on the runway cleared for departure. I made the decision, due to the lack of time, to do the takeoff, and after we climbed out, I would give the jet to him. As I looked down the runway, I was blinded by the runway edge lights and asked the tower to turn them down. Once the lights went out, I pushed the power up, released brakes, and my co-pilot said, "Wow, it's dark!" We climbed out, it hit me like a couple of butterflies in the stomach, and I thought, "Man, that was stupid! What if my NVGs had gone out on T/O roll, and I would have had to give the jet to my co-pilot? Don't we train with both pilots on NVGs?" Now I know why. Is that why the instructor failed my NVGs in the simulator every time I did a T/O?

After we leveled off and were clear of the mountains, I gave the aircraft to the co-pilot and had a long discussion as to why what I did was so stupid. We all agreed. Thanks, guys.

Lessons Learned:

I think you get the picture — go green or go home!

NVGs, when used properly and at the right time, though troublesome, heavy and uncomfortable, could be the saving grace some day.

There would have been nothing wrong with holding at altitude while we put them on and then continuing our descent over the mountains, nor would there have been anything wrong with holding position before T/O and putting them on. There was no inbound or outbound traffic, so what was the hurry?

There isn't anything more important to me now than taking the time to do the right thing at the right time. That is, if I can think of it at the right time! I felt one step behind that whole night, and it's obvious, looking back, that I was.

NOTES:

A LESSON RE-LEARNED
F-16, 61 FIGHTER SQUADRON, LUKE AFB AZ

Captain Dag Grantham, May 2000

Train to recognize your G-tolerance on any given day

"One-point-seven, one-point-six, one-point-five... Brag, FIGHT'S ON!"

One of the greatest peacetime radio calls a fighter pilot will ever hear or say.

It was a gorgeous day in the Republic of Korea (ROK) and I had just received that exact radio call from Brag 02, my wingman. I was the defensive fighter on what I figured would be our last set for the day. I immediately rolled and put my lift vector directly in my wingman's face. I decided to see some out-of-plane offensive maneuvering, so I pulled through a split-S to find him driving to where my turn circle had been just seconds before. We made a right-to-right pass, and he was level-to-slightly-descending as he roared by my right wing 4500 feet away.

After watching him rotate towards me, I knew he was going to drive around my six o'clock position and end up just off my left side at seven to eight o'clock. With just enough energy to make it over the top, I pulled the jet into a barrel roll to the left to maneuver in behind him. I took my eyes off him to start the maneuver, planning to reacquire him as I reached the inverted portion of my barrel roll. Sure enough, I picked him up low and left of my wingtip AIM-9 Sidewinder as I pulled through the vertical.

"Wonder how he'll react to this," I thought as I pulled him to my Heads-Up-Display (HUD). It was then I realized he wasn't reacting—something was wrong.

Continuation Training BFM, it's Friday, and the weather is actually clear and a million (unheard of in the ROK). Oh, did I mention it was a double turn? My wingman and I were scheduled to blast off, fly a sortie of 2v2 Air Combat Maneuvering (ACM) with another flight, hit the flows for some gas, and then off again for some 1v1 BFM. I hadn't flown pure BFM in a few months and with an impending assignment back to the Fighter Training Unit (FTU) at Luke Air Force Base to teach new F-16 pilots, I was looking forward to scraping the rust off my BFM skills. The other flight lead briefed the specifics for the ACM sortie and then my wingman and I got together and ran through a quick brief on how we were going to execute our second sortie. The plan was for me to get three sets as the offensive fighter with a limited thrust bandit, and then give my wingman the remaining sets as the offensive fighter with a more advanced adversary. I briefed my "motherhood" with the following emphasis on G-Awareness:

> "Anti-G Straining Manoeuvre - Standard - expect a 90/180 for air-to-air purposes."

Per AFI 11-114, we needed to get at least one 90° turn and one 180° turn under high G to prepare ourselves mentally and physically for the impending G-load during BFM. We usually defaulted to two 90° turns for our G-awareness prior to the tactical portion of our standard air-to-ground sorties due to our LANTIRN mission, so I emphasised the fact that a 90/180 would be needed instead.

After briefing, we put on our flight gear and stepped on time with the other flight. It is squadron policy to wear the Combat Edge vest as well as the survival vest on all sorties. I was munching on a Power Bar and trying to finish a liter of water as I got off the pilot van at my aircraft. I knew how hot it was outside, and with a double turn running over the lunch hour I was anxious to get some energy in my gut and fill up on water so as not to get dehydrated. The short walk-around was extremely hot with the full complement of Life Support Gear; however, the extra water I drank during the ride to the jet was helping me stay cool.

Start, taxi, takeoff and flight to the area for the first mission were uneventful. The other two-ship flight leader had the lead of both formations and directed two 180° G-awareness turns. After we were set up, we accomplished five 2v2 short-range ACM engagements with relatively little time spent at G higher than 6.5 due to the quick terminates. Both wingmen were performing well as supporting fighters, so the engagements did not last long. After a "bingo" call from my wingman, we departed the airspace and flew an uneventful formation landing. A top-off in the flows, and we were off again to get in our 1v1 BFM time. We had to cruise to an area that was a bit farther away this time, so I was preparing myself to start the fights as expeditiously as possible to maximise training.

Area entry and the G-awareness manoeuvre were uneventful and as briefed. After both calling ready, we began the art that is BFM. The first three sets were uneventful except for my flagrant abuse of standard BFM principles-"Fly to the elbow, not the wrist," I shouted in my mask as we rolled and tumbled through the sky. During his three engagements as the bandit, I limited him to a 90° turn in afterburner before being thrust-limited the rest of the fight. This resulted in him maintaining a relatively low constant G over the duration of several fights. My wingman hadn't pulled excessively high G, but he was getting worn down. I had spent my time on offense long enough, so I told him the next set would be his as we reset the formation after the third terminate call. We both climbed to the initial BFM starting parameters for a 9000-foot perch setup:

Altitude -15,000 +/- 500 ft

Formation - Line abreast, 3000 ft plus the perch (12,000 ft for this engagement)

Airspeed - 425 kts +/- 25 kts at "Fight's on"

I directed him to turn towards me as I subsequently turned away from him. With the Radar Warning Receiver chirping in my ears, I turned back into him, picked him up visually, and listened for him to count down the ranges and call "Fight's on!"

"One-point-seven, one-point-six, one-point-five... Brag, FIGHT'S ON!"

It was then that I realized he wasn't reacting. He should have been planting his lift vector in my face and closing the range between our aircraft. Instead, he was accelerating away from me in a slightly descending flight path. He was at 11,000 feet and I was above him at 13,000. I immediately called for a radio check, but didn't give him any time to answer, because I already knew - he had GLOC'd, and was just a passenger in a fighter that was accelerating downhill at about 10 degrees nose low. I called for a check again and began using his flying callsign, "Brag 2, radio check." With my slow speed over the top, I was rapidly being left behind due to his acceleration. I screamed into the microphone for him to answer, and then switched to his squadron nickname as I changed the emphasis from responding verbally to just pulling up - "(Nickname), pull up." I was unsure how high he was above the water due to the clear day and low wave height. He got almost 1.5 miles in front of me, still going downhill, when I saw the contrails coming off his wing roots—indicative of G on the aircraft at high speed.

At this point he responded that he was pulling up and we knocked off the engagement. I began giving him vectors to base, directed him to go on 100% oxygen, and rejoined on his wing. Once we both calmed down a bit, we declared an emergency and I dropped him off from a straight-in before going around for my own uneventful landing.

Upon review of his tapes, we discovered he had GLOC'd after making two good decisions and one poor one. As he started to enter the turn circle, he got the tunnel vision effect from not being on top of his G-strain, so he released some G to get on top of it. As he started pulling again, he repeated the same sequence of events after getting tunnel vision a second time. At this point, he realised how much of an advantage he was giving me and decided to pull hard to get back into the fight. This last pull overshot his current G-strain and he GLOC'd. He was out for a total of 17 seconds, and when he came to and pulled, he bottomed out at 5500 feet above the ocean while going 630 KCAS! If he had been just a few more degrees nose low, he may have hit the water before those 17 seconds expired.

The effects of G and the need for an effective G-strain are things we brief before every sortie. It's that important in 9 G-or-more capable fighters. Education and training begins at pilot training, extends into Introduction to Fighter Fundamentals (IFF), and on into FTU. By the time a pilot is operational, countless hours have been spent learning how to fly and fight under G. So, how did my wingman GLOC? There are multiple variables that affect one's G tolerance. Some examples are improperly fitted life support equipment, dehydration, lack of high-G sorties in a night squadron, and fatigue after 1.5 high-G sorties.

Lessons Learned:

The lesson re-learned from this GLOC incident is to recognize when your abilities to operate under G are being taxed to their limit. After two attempts at pulling high G and having to come off your fight game plan due to problems with G-tolerance, reassess your ability to fight at that moment. Call for a "knock-it-off" and reset the engagement or try a less G-intensive setup. Also, recheck your life support gear for proper function.

The key word in this incident is training. Use the training you have received to operate under G effectively. Train to recognise warning signs to your G tolerance on any given day. And, finally, realize we are engaged in training each day we fly—not combat. Since it is training , we can afford to bring it home and fly again another day. Check six.

NOTES:

CHAPTER 8
WEATHER & ICING

"There is no reason to fly through a thunderstorm in peacetime."

Sign over squadron ops desk at Davis-Monthan Air Force Base, USAF, AZ, 1970.

COLD WEATHER FLYING

CF-5, AVIATION SAFETY DIVISION, AIR FORCE SAFETY CENTER, KIRTLAND AFB, N.M.

Major Peter Laurin, Winter 2011

Canadian Forces Base Cold Lake, Alberta, Canada, is a winter wonderland in December. One year, the area had received a large amount of snow early in the winter season, and a few winter storms had already hit the base. The holidays were just a few days away, and I was going to celebrate them with my wife and our 9-month-old daughter.

The week before the holidays, our squadron flew regular air-ground missions. Part of the training involved heading to the Jimmy Lake Weapons Range in Alberta for practice weapons delivery. I was No. 3 in a four-ship of CF-5s. We would be flying the first wave to Jimmy Lake, delivering modular practice bombs and CRV-7 rockets and honing our gun-strafing skills. The weather turned out to be perfect that day — clear skies, very light winds and the temperature was 5 below zero. Overnight temperatures were forecast to be minus 12. With these conditions, we were dressed in full winter gear.

All flight planning and preparations were completed, and no alternate was needed; if required, it would have been Edmonton,

Alberta. Edmonton is just over 100 nautical miles to the west-southwest and would have required considerable fuel reserves.

Our four-ship was the first to launch that morning; taking off after us would be CF-18s and the venerable T-33s. On the surface this appeared to be a routine training mission flown by experienced pilots — all had completed at least one tour on the CF-18.

The sortie went as planned; the range work, procedures and radio calls were all completed to perfection. All that remained was to return to base (RTB) via the overhead break and, if gas permitted, a closed pattern or two. This was turning out to be one of those rare, near-perfect missions from start to finish.

On RTB we discovered all was not well at the airfield. As we tried to check in with the air traffic control (ATC) tower, we heard two CF-18s had diverted to Edmonton. The radio was extremely busy and there was much confusion. I distinctly remember hearing, "The airfield is blanketed by ice fog caused by departing CF-18s; all aircraft expect to divert to Edmonton." Conditions favorable for ice fog formation are air temperature below zero, a small temperature dew point spread (less than 2 degrees) and high humidity.

Immediately our four-ship climbed to 20,000 feet and slowed to max endurance. We switched to the instrument flight rules (IFR) recovery frequency. Again, the radio was busy with aircraft trying to recover to the base. We couldn't get a response from ATC since they were overwhelmed with IFR traffic. We knew our situation was bad, but not yet dire. We couldn't divert to Edmonton — Cold Lake was our only option. To make matters worse, the CF-5 had no instrument landing system (ILS) capability; we were PAR (precision approach radar) only for precision approaches at a Category E speed.

We held at max endurance and continued calling out to ATC. After what seemed like an inordinate amount of time, ATC directed their attention to us. At this point we had enough gas for only one approach, and our section was split into elements. On the radio we continued to hear that aircraft were diverting to Edmonton. The situation was now dire.

I knew from experience that PAR recoveries never put the CF-5 in a good position to land from decision height (DH). We usually ended up off-centerline or slightly high. The PAR controllers tried their best but, in the last two miles of the approach, the speed of the CF-5 caused the PAR controllers to fall behind on their corrections. I knew I had to fly a perfect PAR approach with careful attention paid to glide path calls. I couldn't do anything to correct for centerline errors other than follow the controllers' instructions.

As I led the second element, I had the benefit of hearing how the first element was being controlled. Unfortunately, and as expected, in the last two miles of their approach, I could sense the PAR controller was struggling. When the controller asked for our missed approach request, I heard a distinct change in the controller's voice when we requested ejection vectors as our missed approach.

Canadian Forces Base Cold Lake has two parallel runways. The inner runway is the longer of the two and is the dedicated IFR runway while the outer is for visual flight rules traffic. The lead element was approaching DH for the approach. As I listened carefully, I heard lead call "Visual between the runways; two take spacing." No. 2 very wisely not only took spacing, but immediately moved over to land on the outer runway as this was the closest runway to him and, due to IFR conditions, he knew the runway wasn't being used. This was an excellent decision as it allowed each pilot to land and use drag chutes to decelerate if necessary.

I expected the same situation would repeat itself for my element. We ended up at a similar DH between the runways. Like the element in front of us, I took the inner runway and my wingman landed on the outer runway — a successful ending to our mission.

Lessons Learned:

I was reminded of a few valuable lessons on that cold, December day:

1. Everyone in aviation must work together; if something changes, like the weather, notify all concerned.
2. Our formation should have requested priority from ATC.
3. Cold weather flying requires proper preparations — respect the elements!

NOTES:

ICED UP

EC-130H, OPERATIONAL INFORMATION WITHHELD

Name withheld by request, Nov 2008

It was 10 minutes before arriving on station for my crew's last combat sortie of the deployment. We'd started picking up some light, mixed icing about 15 minutes earlier, and this was pretty normal during our last few sorties. Another night of icing meant extra vigilance to back up our Herc's automatic ice-detection and deicing systems. Just before we ran our combat-entry checklist, the co-pilot kicked off one of the most exciting 30 minutes I have flown in an EC-130H. "Hey, Eng," he said, "are you sure the prop anti-icing is working?"

In C-130s, we use engine bleed air to keep our engines and wing and empennage leading edges ice-free. Electric elements heat the propellers, pitot tubes and windscreen. These systems easily cleared the kind of trace and light icing our crew had experienced so far.

This night was different, though. While the engineer double-checked the de-icing power flowing to the props, the precipitation outside grew heavier. Although we verified our icing systems were operational, that was our first clue that this icing was different from the nights before. The next indication came when the flashlights we were using to check the propellers flashed across the ice building up on the windscreen, despite the windows' internal heating elements.

Since our onboard systems couldn't keep up with the unforecast icing in our fragged airspace, we needed to arrange a new block or go home. Just like in training, we delegated our crew duties and began to solve our problem. The co-pilot continued to fly, my navigator focused on his weather radar to find us a clear patch of air, and the engineer and extra navigator scanned the engines and wings to keep track of the accumulating ice. We were already operating at our cruise ceiling, so I radioed Centre to let them know we would need a descent of 5,000 feet to get clear of the severe icing. The descent still left us above the freezing level, and although the icing was not as dramatic, our systems still couldn't keep up. With no hope of operating in our planned airspace, we turned 180 degrees back toward the clear air we had come from, and our de-icing systems finally started to catch up.

With the situation marginally under control, I radioed the local Metro station. The meteorologists didn't have much new info for us, except that the existing weather conditions were not forecasted to change anytime soon. I filed a quick PIREP to keep other aircraft out of the mess that night.

The navigator's radar indicated that our only chance for finding clearer air where we could employ our weapons system was about 10 minutes away at the western end of our orbit. We weren't yet ready to abandon our fragged support for the Army, so I coordinated with Center for a climb to the west. During our climb, the co-pilot reported that the aircraft's performance was beginning to suffer — despite max power, we were rapidly losing our ability to climb. Once again, just before arriving on track, our de-icing systems began to fall behind, forcing us to descend and turn back toward home.

Although we felt good giving the Army our best effort, it was clear that Mother Nature didn't want us flying our mission that "dark and stormy night." Now, we had to get home.

By then, we'd descended below our tactically safe altitude. No big deal in the clouds where nobody could see us, but we wanted to climb on our way home across the clearer skies of central Iraq. As the co-pilot added power and raised the nose to climb, the whole plane began a slow, hammering buffet at our charted four-engine climb speed that none of us had ever felt before. This was the first time we realised how much ice we'd be carrying home with us. Although we could see the inches of ice on some of our nonheated leading edges, like the external fuel tanks, we now realized that the dozens of antennas we use for our mission were carrying too much ice to climb even from these medium altitudes.

We quickly plotted a new route home to avoid the highest threat areas of Iraq and began to consider our approach to our base. As dawn crept across the sky, we were able to see the extent of icing on our plane. Antennas and unheated windows were coated with chunky mixed ice more than four inches deep. With hundreds of pounds of ice clinging to our plane's nose, external fuel tanks and dozens of extra antennas, we knew we needed to thaw out before we slowed and configured for landing. We executed an en route descent over the unpopulated desert along the Kuwaiti border and began to melt the glacier that had built up on our nose and antennas. When the football-sized chunks of ice finally stopped breaking loose and dramatically flying past our windows, we completed our descent and final approach for a safe landing.

This mission taught me a dangerous lesson about icing: don't delay the decision to fly out of icing conditions. Although our heavy, high-drag EC-130H didn't have the performance to climb to the clear air just a couple thousand feet above, we shouldn't have hesitated to descend and turn toward clearer air.

How much icing is too much in the C-130? From now on, I'll be alert for the two most obvious signs: ice building up on prop spinners and ice building up on the windscreen. We demonstrated that the C-130's wing and empennage anti-icing system is powerful enough to keep up with even severe icing. However, if prop de-icing and windscreen heat cannot keep up with ice, the crew cannot afford to delay maneuvering clear of the icing. Every moment you press into icing conditions may cost you hundreds or thousands of feet of service ceiling. Even in aircraft without the EC-130H's generous ice-collecting surfaces, there are too many fairings, pods and antennas that can accumulate dangerous icing.

Lessons Learned:

Good CRM made the difference for our crew. We clearly designated who was responsible for flying, radios, weather radar, de-icing systems and visually monitoring ice build-up. Each crew member contributed to our successful recovery by making clear, assertive statements about the weather radar picture, the "feel" of the flight controls, and observations of ice building up on our special system antennas.

Collectively, we were able to make informed decisions and safely recover from a dangerous situation none of us had experienced before.

NOTES:

COLD, WET AND HEAVY
C-130, OPERATIONAL INFORMATION WITHHELD

Name withheld by request, Nov 2008

There are some days as a flyer when I feel satisfied that I've fully prepared for a day's sortie. I've also had days when things began to fall apart, the crew wasn't hitting on all cylinders, lead telling me I was out of position, I wasn't anticipating what was next, and I was holding onto the tail of the aircraft trying to claw my way back in. We've all had that feeling of being behind the aircraft, and as professional aviators, we try to ensure those days of big power inputs and low SA get fewer and far between. When I think of why we get behind the aircraft, there's one reason that stands out more than the rest: complacency.

Our Air Force has a culture of working smarter and not harder, seeking to maximize efficiency and minimize workload. This has resulted in many of the mission-planning aspects of a sortie being delegated to other entities. Mission-planning cells present us with our mission information pre-canned for each tactical sortie, and tanker/airlift control centre flight managers produce mission materials, akin to mission-planning fast food. Although it's the responsibility of the aircraft commander to ensure that the materials are correct, it's all too easy to trust the materials with a cursory check when pressed for time and to become complacent in preparing for flight.

It was an early Sunday morning, about 4:30 a.m., when I just finished alerting my crew for the day's flight. As I threw my break bag together and stepped out the door, I was greeted with six inches of snow covering my boot and rising above my ankle. As far as I knew, it didn't snow too often at my new duty station, maybe twice a year at the most. About the time that I threw my bag into the back seat of my car, the duty officer called stating that maintenance wanted to know if we were going to take off and if they should prepare the aircraft for flight. Murphy's Law was gaining momentum. That the aircraft wasn't being prepared for flight, and that I was receiving a phone call, meant that we were behind schedule already. We'd have to hustle to take off in time to stay on frag for the next day of our three-country, three-day trip. Arriving at the squadron, I delegated tasks as we signed in and prepared for flight. The co-pilot printed the flight manager prepared mission materials, the navigator checked the routing, and the rest of the crew began the preflight and loaded the aircraft.

I finished filing the paperwork and checked on the progress of the rest of the crew, and then went with the co-pilot and another crew member to Base Ops to check on the weather. The weather briefer gave us our -1, pre-filled, and asked if we had any questions after looking at it. We checked the radar picture, noted our probable flight level winds, and briefly noted any problem areas. I asked the weather briefer if there was severe icing, and he noted that there was probably some light-to-moderate icing because of the snow. Satisfied with his answer, we left, gathered our gear and proceeded to the aircraft.

After a three-hour delay due to airfield plowing operations, maintenance delays, poor visibility, loading delays, loading reconfiguration, the de-icing truck breaking, the de-icing truck getting fixed, then running out of fluid, being refilled, and then successfully de-icing the aircraft, we were ready to kick this pig and get on the road. At this point, I can say that I had channelized my attention on just getting the aircraft off the ground. And in our military's present state of operating aging aircraft, most flyers can identify with these challenges.

However, the challenges for my crew that day had only begun after we ensured the exceptional release was signed. Each crew member made last minute checks as we approached the hold short line and called ready for takeoff. We were the only show in town since it was a Sunday, so we were sure that we'd receive clearance rather quickly. Sure enough, the clearance came; we checked the RVR to make sure that we were legal and positioned the aircraft for takeoff. At this point, the flight engineer stated that he was turning on the anti-icing and de-icing systems, since it was still snowing and we had a thick deck of clouds to go through. I acknowledged his statement and stated, "Roger."

As I applied power, I noticed a slight decrease in performance of the engines due to the anti-icing systems, but all within expectations of performance. The aircraft pulled away from the concrete runway and lugged into the clouds at 400 feet AGL. There was no break in the weather as the aircraft passed 10,000 feet MSL, and the co-pilot checked the oxygen system and the cabin altitude. All was as it should be. We could hear the precipitation hitting the aircraft and began accumulating icing at 12,000 feet MSL.

Still in the weather with no probability of breaking out for another 6,000 feet, an insidious change in the aircraft's performance began. The climb rate slowed, controls became sluggish, and I had to keep a higher nose high attitude to continue the climb. Yet, there were no visual clues to validate what I was seeing on the leading edge of the wing and what I thought was happening. Ultimately, the plane had a higher deck angle than normal, we couldn't reach our calculated altitude, and our VVI was now zero. Now that we were past the terrain, I commanded the co-pilot to request an immediate descent due to icing. The center complied, and we began a descent to 10,000 feet. For the next hour, we ran our anti-icing and de-icing systems continuously until all the ice had melted.

Knowing that fuel was now becoming a factor and being in a position to climb once again, we requested and received a clearance to climb to our final altitude. This time the aircraft made it, and we were able to get on top of the cloud deck. At level-off and acceleration, the additional crew member said that he had calculated that we were plus four minutes on gas to make it to our destination with the necessary reserves. I checked fuel quantity, fuel flow and ground speed, and was satisfied with his calculation. Yet, there was something nagging in my mind. I checked fuel again, ran fuel-consumption calculations, and with our groundspeed affected by the 125-knot wind on our nose, we weren't going to make it with our necessary reserves. I stated my calculations to the crew, had someone else confirm the calculations, and then set a bingo for diverting to an alternate field for fuel.

Ultimately, we reached bingo fuel, diverted, refuelled and proceeded on to our destination and continued the mission, but one thing was clear from this experience: I was complacent. Although no disaster occurred, it very easily could have because I didn't do the proper pre-mission planning to ensure that I operated the aircraft and the crew in the safest manner. As the aircraft commander, I am responsible, period. It's a simple fact that is easy to forget, but being responsible means being prepared and taking the steps necessary, however inconvenient, to take care of the crew and the mission.

Lessons Learned:

Would I have taken off again? Yes, I would have, and I would be blowing smoke to say that I wouldn't have. But one of the biggest lessons I gleaned from this experience was that pre-mission TOLD can make a difference in departure planning. Sure, as aviators we may think about losing an engine and the steps we would take in a high, hot and heavy situation, but not too often do we think about the decrease in performance that can occur in cold, wet and heavy conditions. Icing is insidious and doesn't always provide the visual cues we often look for to validate what we're seeing on our performance instruments in the plane. Icing is also cumulative. The longer one stays in icing conditions, the worse it is. The aircraft's weight increases, aerodynamics change and stall speeds increase.

I could have done a better job in pre-mission planning by asking about the freezing level, comparing that to the cloud thickness, time-to-climb calculations, and calculating correctly the service ceiling, fuel flow, and TAS effects of operating the anti-icing/de-icing systems. I could have done all of this the day before the mission.

It's easy to be complacent when it comes to performance. We operate within our respective MWS's envelope and notice small changes at the margins. But it's the margins that can make a difference in an emergency or critical situation. As we move out of the winter season and into the spring and summer, icing can still be a factor. More than likely, you may find yourself in that high, hot and heavy situation. Take the time and run some numbers, plan for the most inopportune time, and find those margins.

NOTES:

THUNDERSTORMS

T-1A JAYHAWK TRAINER, OPERATIONAL
INFORMATION WITHHELD

Name withheld by request, Nov 2008

Seventeen days after becoming a qualified instructor pilot in the T-1A, I experienced a sortie I'd never forget. As a second lieutenant first assignment instructor pilot, I had no illusions I'd be prepared for any situation. I did, however, assume I would gain moderate experience before that preparation would come into question. One day, I was scheduled to fly with a student on a 2.0 navigation sortie to Amarillo, Texas. There were some possible thunderstorms in the area, but our intended route of flight was forecast clear.

During the benign cruise flight from Vance Air Force Base, Oklahoma, I attempted to install as much wisdom an 18-month aviator could possibly install into a student who'd already flown commercially and had been flying far longer than I had. We worked in the Amarillo traffic pattern with my flight commander and one of our check pilots. We all kept watch on storms building to the north and south of our route back. About halfway through our intended training, the convective situation started to worsen. We made the conservative decision to return, not wanting to push our luck with the weather. All three planes got the same clearance back to Vance; we departed last.

Flying back, I was able to track the other two airplanes via our traffic/collision avoidance system. We were routed through Gage, a navaid, where we make an easterly turn toward Vance. We could see the thunderstorms building to the south and north. I was excited, as this provided ample opportunity to show off the features of the weather radar to the student. I knew the T-1A was one of the more advanced airplanes with its avionics and displays. It has an all-glass cockpit, so all my displays were digital and vastly superior to every other airplane I'd ever flown. I wasn't worried about the build-up, as we were right behind a flight commander and a check pilot. Everything must be OK. We were all talking on the common frequency, aware of where the storms were and which way they were building. The other two pilots didn't sound concerned, so neither was I.

Making the turn at Gage, we were able to get a clear picture of what was happening. I was "painting" completely red to the north and south, with centers of magenta. The magenta color told me we were dealing with some very real thunderstorms. I had been taught that magenta was the worst of the worst when it came to "painting" convective activity. The red was also severe enough to be avoided at any cost. With some minor deviations, I was still "painting" green for a route into Vance. As my flight commander asked for a deviation, followed by the check pilot, I followed suit. They both flew through the middle of the area I was "painting" green.

Continuing east toward Vance, we penetrated the green; we were in solid IMC but no precipitation. I was still "painting" green all the way to Vance, with red and magenta to the north and south. That was when it happened, immediately and without warning. The noise was deafening.

We immediately lost the ability to hear anyone over our radios. The pitot static instruments became completely erratic. The altimeter and airspeed indicators were rapidly spinning up and down, with the vertical velocity indicator showing random climbs and descents in the thousands of feet per minute. This was about the time I made the biggest mistake of my flying career: I looked outside my window and aft. To that point, I had no idea how much a wing could actually flex in the vertical. They no longer looked like a soaring bird's wings. They were now big flapping pieces of metal that looked more like a guy riding a unicycle off a cliff with homemade wings of paper and wood, flapping madly to stay airborne.

In retrospect, it seems like I watched those wings for hours, anticipating the inevitable snapping of metal. In reality, it was only a second, as almost every warning horn was going off in the airplane. Then I heard a new warning — the one you get when throttles are pulled back and the gear is not down. That one got my attention. The student, still flying, had the instinctive reaction to pull power off as the gauges showed a massive descent and airspeed going above the operational limit of the airplane. As I had more free brain cells at the moment than she did, I realized the last thing we wanted to do was take any power away from the airplane.

I took the airplane, pushed the throttles back up, and attempted to take stock of the situation. I'd always been taught that once you're in a storm, it's generally better to find the quickest way out in the general direction you're going. The alternative of turning around would take you a few more miles into the storm, only to reverse course and retrace those miles out, usually keeping you in the storm longer. That was when it occurred to me that it was still not raining! Well, not raining water, anyway — it was raining huge masses of ice. I remember seeing what looked like tennis ball-sized pieces of ice. In reality, they were probably more like golf balls. I then noticed what looked like worse conditions ahead, including lightning. I made the decision to turn around and get out of the hail. As I did this, I made a radio call to ATC, heard by the other T-1.

As I was yelling, "I'M TURNING AROUND!", I never did hear ATC, and we had to yell in the cockpit just to hear each other. I'll never forget that turn. I had a pit in my stomach as we continued to get pummelled. Once I'd made the decision, there was no going back, and we would soon find out if it was the right decision.

We got turned around, and at some point the pummelling ceased. Soon thereafter, our instruments came back, and we could hear ATC again. As things settled down, we realized we came out more than 5,000 feet lower than we went into the weather. We spent another 45 minutes attempting to work our way into Vance or find a VMC hole to Wichita, Kan. I was unwilling to go into IMC again, regardless of ATC assurances that it was clear of storms.

We eventually landed uneventfully, and everything seemed fine until I taxied into parking. It wasn't until I saw the looks on the faces of every crew chief and maintainer, as they waved anyone nearby over to look, that I realized I'd made a mistake. I never declared an emergency, so no one was expecting a damaged airplane. I didn't need traffic priority as I was getting all the ATC attention I wanted. It wasn't a conscious decision — it was oversight. I quickly got out of the airplane to look. I don't know what I expected, but seeing the damage on an airplane you just landed hits you a certain way. The leading edges were all dented, some flattened; the nose cone looked as if it had been sandblasted; the pylons holding the engines on were simply beaten; a quarter of one windshield wiper was broken off; and the GPS antenna was smashed.

The rest of the day consisted of paperwork, and eventually, a private meeting with the operations officer. Of all the lessons I learned, one was definitely an example of how a great leader handles this type of situation. He took me into his office, and he asked me about the radar and weather. When he was satisfied I knew the things I was supposed to know, he ensured I was on the schedule to fly the next day. He told me very succinctly what he thought about our attempt to "shoot the gap," and he was disappointed that I didn't declare an emergency. Aside from that, he made it a learning experience for a very new pilot.

Lessons Learned:

Another important lesson I learned was just because someone has more experience, higher rank or a command position in the squadron doesn't mean blindly following or agreeing with a decision they make is OK. They may have made the best decision for their aircraft, but I was in charge of my aircraft and owed it to myself and my student to ensure it was the best decision for us, as well.

The lessons learned that day will not be forgotten. Not by me, my student or anyone else who was around to see that airplane, or our faces when we returned.

NOTES:

COMMON SENSE

C-21 SUPER TAXI, OPERATIONAL INFORMATION WITHHELD

Name withheld by request, Nov 2008

"Operational risk management!" Ha, what a joke. Are all these guidelines really designed to help keep me, God's gift to aviation and the Air Force, extra safe? Or are they just to help increase the rate at which we destroy forests and to give me extra paperwork? Why does someone like me, fresh from the best pilot training program available, need to worry about extra stuff like that? All I need are the keys and I'm good to go. That's what I thought about a year ago. Soon I'd find how useful ORM is in every situation as a final safety check of your common sense.

When I first arrived at my unit, I was on top of the world — shiny silver wings blazing across my chest, a new wife prettier than a sunset over the Rocky Mountains, and my ego, barely able to fit through the door. I knew how to take off and land, figuring that was all there was to UPT. I figured that was all there was to flying any jet.

On my first mission in the sleek C-21 Super Taxi, I was along mainly to load bags and see how a mission was run operationally. What we do on the road is what everybody learned to do in T1s: take off, full stop somewhere else, pick up a pax or two, fly somewhere else, and continue until done. Pretty simple. My first assumption is generally correct; our missions normally go as planned, without a hitch. Every once in a while a problem creeps in, and the chain begins.

We arrived at the first stop on time and dropped off the Space-A passengers and went in for the base ops drill. We flew over some T-storms on the way in, but those shouldn't have been a factor, because we were scheduled to take off in 40 minutes, and the storms were about two hours out. We had one duty pax waiting in the DV lounge, and another was running late. So we waited and kept checking the thunderstorms, and waited some more. Now we were out at the jet waiting with the GPU running. Two hours passed and those T-storms were then overhead, so we went back inside and started checking our crew duty time. It looked like we'd make it home, but just barely if we took off in the next hour. The final pax showed, but then there was lightning within five miles. We then got a call that we were cleared for takeoff. We scratched our heads and wondered how lightning within 5 miles could be "waived," so we talked to weather to see what was up. We found out that it was safe to head out to the jet, and our escape route through the storms was to the south, which was where we were headed. We pressed.

The GPU was running and we started to crank engines, when we noticed the GPU was off line and our AC unit had been running the whole time, draining the batteries. The engine started, but the batteries overheated. We had to shut down, go back inside and wait for maintenance to replace the batteries. Another two hours passed and we knew we probably weren't going home that night, since we were going to run out of crew duty day.

Our day kept getting worse. The pax was restless, because our final lift, the one who arrived for an on-time takeoff, couldn't go to his final destination because it had closed two hours before. We had to off-load him where his car wasn't, and the lift who arrived two hours late was mad, because now he was five hours late. Either way, we weren't having a good time anymore. In the end, everything worked out ... no emergencies. We got everybody where they needed to be, albeit a little late, and maybe a little bit farther from home than they would've liked, but home, nonetheless, and home safely. This is because of our common sense and good ORM skills.

How did ORM filter into any of this? I never once mentioned that we filled out an ORM worksheet. ORM is a continuing process, used very much like common sense to filter out what you should be doing or what you could do to mitigate associated hazards and risks. One obvious hazard and associated risk in this situation was the thunderstorms.

The ORM loop has us look at six things to determine what should be done:

- Identify the hazards
- Assess the risk
- Analyze risk control factors
- Make control decisions
- Implement risk control
- Supervise and evaluate

Hazard identification was easy: thunderstorms.

The assessed risk is getting struck by lightning or crashing due to wind shear. Along with assessing the risk, we look at how long we'd be exposed to the danger. Being exposed to lightning on the ramp and in the air is the greatest threat, because of time and the ability of a Learjet to be able to fly through wind shear on takeoff. In analyzing risk control factors, we determined the best solution was not to go onto the ramp with lightning, and delayed due to weather. Deciding and implementing happened almost simultaneously for us, as we were the ones with the authority to decide if we would enter the ramp. Evaluating later was easy, as we still completed the mission, just a little later.

Lessons Learned:

The process isn't complicated and isn't a waste of time. You do it every day for every action. It's simply common sense. ORM is the name of the process for common sense. Does it waste time, paper and money? No. It's just another tool you can use to help make things easier and less stressful when things go awry.

NOTES:

COUGAR 21
C-130, 40 AS/DOFA DYESS AFB, TX

Captain Ronald A. Bottoms, May 2008

"Cougar 21, confirm you have landed; tower does not have visual."

I looked over at the aircraft commander, took a deep breath, and replied "Affirmative."

"OK, take the next taxiway to your left and tell us which one it is; we will send a follow-me out to help you taxi to parking."

You might be asking, "What was keeping the tower from seeing a C-130 sitting on its runway?" Answer — the visibility was somewhere between 100 and 150 feet due to early morning fog. A gray C-130 tends to blend in well with gray fog.

The day started out with a simple mission: carry a maintenance rescue team and another crew from Little Rock Air Force Base, Ark. to Alexandria International, La., wait around for a few hours to see if the MRT could fix the aircraft that was stuck at Alexandria, and then return to Little Rock. Just an easy air land mission, right? Nobody shooting at us, no low-level flying, no need to max-perform the aircraft; just go from point A to point B and return. We didn't even need to refuel once we landed; the round-trip flight was well within the standard fuel load for a C-130. It was a gorgeous night for flying; we could see a million stars as we flew south. What could go wrong?

We had no problems loading the aircraft, made an on-time takeoff, and landed at Alexandria International uneventfully. After offloading the MRT, we went inside to recheck the weather and NOTAMs and settled down to wait. And wait. And wait some more. After six hours, we had to make a decision on whether to proceed back to Little Rock without the other crew and the MRT. You see, the MRT was unable to duplicate the electrical problem on the other aircraft, described by another crew as a lightning bolt going off underneath the flight deck. The extra crew decided not to fly the other aircraft back at night, so we loaded up everyone and headed back to Little Rock, planning to land right after dawn. Did we miss anything? We had enough fuel to make it back, and we had checked our weather and NOTAMs. Our divert base was Adams Field, only about 15 minutes from the base. No problem, except that it was late fall, we were planning to land right after dawn, we only had about 30 minutes of extra fuel, and our weather forecast was already six hours old when we took off for Little Rock.

The return trip was uneventful until just before we started our descent, when Little Rock approach asked us what our intentions were. Fog had rolled in, covering the area like one of those thick, fluffy white bath towels your mother always kept for guest use only and yelled at you every time you pulled it out of the hall closet. Adams Field was 0/0; nothing was moving. Approach told us the base weather report was calling for a 200-foot ceiling and ½-mile visibility, but kind of chuckled when he said it. I would have laughed too, except I looked at the fuel gauge and realized that we had no choice; we didn't have enough fuel to divert anywhere else.

What do you do in a situation like this? Because of some bad decisions earlier in the night, we had no choice: we shot the approach. The AC told me to fly the ILS; he would look for the field. Once he spotted the field, he would take over for the landing. I was supposed to stay on the instruments, in case we had to go missed approach. The flight engineer would back us up on our airspeed and altitude, and the navigator would monitor the approach. The loadmaster? He just buckled his seat belt really tight.

Everyone knew their duties, and we were ready to start the approach. There was no wind, and I had that approach shacked. Truthfully, I believe it was the best ILS I'd ever flown. It was a good thing, too. Two hundred feet above decision height — no airfield. OK, no big deal, just keep going. One hundred feet above, same thing. I'm a little nervous now. Fifty feet — nothing. Decision height — no one says anything. This is not good. Fifty feet below decision height, 150 feet above the field. I can't stand it anymore. As I began to say, "Crew, we're going around," the AC interrupts with, "I have the lights, my aircraft." I looked outside and could just barely make out the flashing sequencer lights. I didn't see the runway itself, until just before we crossed the threshold, about 75 feet AGL.

The landing was uneventful, as was everything thereafter. The follow-me vehicle found us and led us to parking without incident. Everyone let out a big sigh of relief once we shut down in parking without any bent metal. We managed not to declare emergency fuel, and better yet, we weren't broken into thousands of burning pieces scattered over the Arkansas countryside.

Lessons Learned:

First, checking the weather is not something you just pay lip service to; always get the most current weather possible.

Next, really think about your alternate. Some place 15 minutes away works if the runway is shut down for an IFE, but what if the weather shuts down everything within a 300-mile radius?

Finally, never get complacent. I mean never get complacent.

Aviation is dangerous enough when everything is going right; never give Murphy an edge. He doesn't need it — you do.

NOTES:

CHAPTER 9
FLIGHT ENVELOPE

"I was always afraid of dying. Always. It was my fear that made me learn everything I could about my airplane and my emergency equipment, and kept me flying respectful of my machine and always alert in the cockpit."

Brigadier General Chuck Yeager, USAF

THE YA-HA MANOEUVRE
F-15, OPERATIONAL INFORMATION WITHHELD

Name withheld by request, Dec 1980

The range training officer had just advised me that I had killed the last of four adversary aircraft my element had engaged on a dissimilar air combat tactics mission on an air combat maneuvering instrumentation (ACMI) range. No shots had been fired by the opposition, and I was feeling rather good about how things had gone for me and my Eagle jet.

Partly out of sheer exuberance and partly for the benefit of my A-4 "partner" who had acted as a six-checker while I worked the F-15's radar and weapons systems heavily, I figured one victory roll for each of the four kills I'd been credited with by the ACMI computer would be in order.

So, here goes...stick forward slightly to 1 G, or a touch less, out of the mild climb I was in, then stick smartly to the right, being careful not to go to max deflection (a Dash One no-no in the Eagle if rolling more than 360°). One, two, (going almost too fast to count)...say, the nose is starting to move off its point, three...my God—I'd better knock this off...four...stick is centered laterally but the bird won't quit rolling!...Let's try just a touch of opposite aileron...No good, perhaps increase the roll rate...You dummy, you must have induced an auto-roll...Let's see—are we positive or negative G? Damn, can't tell... Would estimate about 1/2 positive G 'cause I'm light in the seat but not hanging in the straps...Okay, positive—here goes anti-roll rudder.... Jeez! That was obviously the wrong way. The roll rate is at least as fast as, even seems faster (...must have done 8 or 9 rolls by now and the nose is starting to drop below the horizon), but now I'm definitely negative G—the shoulder straps are cutting deep and the lap belt hurts. I guess that's good news. No doubt in my mind now which rudder to use...here goes.

Pro-roll rudder...It's still rolling. I believe it's rolling faster, but I know I've got the correct rudder in...Hope it works, would sure ruin my day if it doesn't...Okay! It's slowing down its roll rate—looks like three rolls after getting all the pro-roll rudder I could achieve...Oops! What was that? As the Eagle stopped its rolling it did a negative 2 1/2 G and a positive 7.3-G ya-ha maneuver with several smaller cycles of the same porpoise-all with the stick held centered. Thank God it's over.

After looking my beast over to ensure all was well, I decided I'd probably not do that again. I distinctly recall thinking how foolish I'd feel if I had rolled that way after splashing my fourth or fifth Flogger only to leap out because I couldn't recover from a condition I had induced.

I've since talked with a senior MACAIR test pilot and a USAF "golden arm" who has flown Eagles since the early days at Edwards. Both stated they'd never been in that particular flight regime, though the MACAIR pilot stated that he was aware of a great dislike by the Eagle for any high, sustained roll rates at negative, or even low angles of attack (the Dash One says so, too).

Flight conditions were approximately 400 KCAS, FL 230, approx .5 G, rapid roll rates. Roll-yaw coupling was apparent by the third roll. Approximate time of "maneuver" was 6 seconds. Best guess on total number of rolls was 12 to 14, altitude loss was 3,500 feet, and airspeed decreased approximately 50 knots. All three control augmentation systems (CAS) axes dropped off during the recovery. Internal wing fuel was within 50 pounds of balanced. I had 5,000 pounds of fuel remaining and a centerline tank.

Lessons Learned:

Further study of the flight manual's Flight Characteristics section convinced me I really hadn't had an "auto-roll" as defined there (it always is a result of high AOA) but, rather, had experienced a particularly nifty example of roll and yaw coupling due to high roll rate, high airspeed, and very low angle of attack. I learned that waiting until coupling becomes evident may well be too late.

I hope the telling of this experience may keep some other aggressively exuberant Eagle driver from being an unwitting and unwilling passenger for one devil of a ride.

NOTES:

CHAPTER 10
FURTHER READING

If you enjoyed reading *81 Lessons From The Sky*, then you might also enjoy the other books in the *Lessons From The Sky* series.

61 Lessons From The Sky (Military Helicopters)
71 Lessons From The Sky (Civilian Helicopters)
81 Lessons From The Sky (General Aviation)
101 Lessons From The Sky (Commercial Aviation)
Top Gun Lessons From The Sky (US Navy)

Do you have any lessons you would like to share with Fletcher, and the aviation community? Email them to Fletcher at **fletch@avgas-group.com** for him to share on his social media accounts, or to include in a future book. Please note that if you do send through any lessons, you are giving us permission to publish those stories.

GLOSSARY

A

ACFT – Aircraft
A1C – Airman First Class; enlisted pay grade E-3, known as Airman Second Class (A2C) from 1952 to 1967
A2C – Airman Second Class; former enlisted pay grade E-3 from 1952 to 1967, now designated as A1C
A3C – Airman Third Class; former enlisted pay grade E-2 from 1952 to 1967, now designated as Amn
AADS – Alaskan Air Defense Sector
AAFES – Army and Air Force Exchange Service (pronounced "A-Fees")
AB – Airman Basic; enlisted pay grade E-1
AB – Air Base
ABDR – Aircraft Battle Damage Repair
ABM – Air Battle Manager
ABU – Airman Battle Uniform
ABW – Air Base Wing
ACA – Airspace Control Authority

ACC – Air Combat Command, also Area Control Center
ACO – Aerospace Control Officer
ACOT – Advanced Communications Officer Training
ACSC – Air Command and Staff College
ACW – Air Control Wing
ADC – Area Defense Counsel
ADC – (Obsolete term) Air Defense Command, later Aerospace Defense Command (disestablished MAJCOM)
ADCON – Administrative Control
ADP – Airman Development Plan
ADPE – Automated Data Processing Equipment
ADR – Airfield Damage Repair
ADSC – Active Duty Service Commitment
AEF – Aerospace Expeditionary Force
AES – Aeromedical Evacuation Squadron
AETC – Air Education and Training Command
AEW – Air Expeditionary Wing
AFA – Air Force Academy
AFA – Air Force Association
AFAA – Air Force Audit Agency
AFAM – Air Force Achievement Medal
AFAMS – Air Force Agency for Modeling and Simulation
Air Force Base – Air Force Base
AFC2IC – Air Force Command and Control Integration Center
AFCA – Air Force Communications Agency
AFCAA – Air Force Cost Analysis Agency
AFCAT – Air Force Catalog
AFCEC – Air Force Civil Engineering Center
AFCEE – Air Force Center for Engineering and the Environment
AFCENT – Air Forces Central
AFCESA – Air Force Civil Engineer Support Agency
AFCFM – Air Force Career Field Manager
AFCLC – Air Force Culture and Learning Center
AFCM – Air Force Commendation Medal

AFDC – Air Force Doctrine Center
AFDW – Air Force District of Washington
AFE – Aircrew Flight Equipment
AFETS – Air Force Engineering and Technical Services
AFFMA – Air Force Frequency Management Agency
AFFSA – Air Force Flight Standards Agency
AFFSC – Air Force Financial Services Center
AFGSC – Air Force Global Strike Command
AFH – Air Force Handbook
AFHRA – Air Force Historical Research Agency
AFI – Air Force Instruction; or as a duty status, awaiting further instructions
AFIA – Air Force Inspection Agency
AFIAA – Air Force Intelligence Analysis Agency
AFIS – Air Force Inspection System
AFISRA – Air Force Intelligence, Surveillance and Reconnaissance Agency
AFIT – Air Force Institute of Technology
AFLC – Air Force Logistics Command (disestablished MAJCOM; merged with AFSC in 1992 to form AFMC)
AFLMA – Air Force Logistics Management Agency
AFLOA – Air Force Legal Operations Agency
AFMA – Air Force Manpower Agency
AFMAN – Air Force Manual
AFMC – Air Force Materiel Command
AFMOA – Air Force Medical Operations Agency
AFMPC – Air Force Military Personnel Center (obsolete), replaced with AFPC
AFMS – Air Force Medical Service or Air Force Manpower Standards
AFMSA – Air Force Medical Support Agency
AFNIC – Air Force Network Integration Center
AFNOC – Air Force Network Operations Center
AFNORTH – Air Forces Northern

AFNSEPO – Air Force National Security Emergency Preparedness Office
AFNWCA – Air Force Nuclear Weapons and Counterproliferation Agency
AFOG – Air Force Operations Group
AFOQT – Air Force Officer Qualifying Test
AFOTEC – Air Force Operational Test and Evaluation Center
AFPAA – Air Force Public Affairs Agency
AFPAM – Air Force Pamphlet
AFPC – Air Force Personnel Center
AFPCA – Air Force Pentagon Communications Agency
AFPD – Air Force Policy Directive
AFPEO – Air Force Program Executive Office
AFPET – Air Force Petroleum Agency
AFPOA – Air Force Personnel Operations Agency
AFRBA – Air Force Review Boards Agency
AFRC – Air Force Reserve Command
AFRIMS – Air Force Records Information Management System
AFRL – Air Force Research Lab
AFROTC – Air Force Reserve Officers Training Corps
AFRPA – Air Force Real Property Agency
AFS – Air Force Station
AFSA – Air Force Sergeants Association
AFSC - Air Force Sustainment Center The mission of the Air Force Sustainment Center is to Sustain Weapon System Readiness to generate Air power for America. The center provides war-winning expeditionary capabilities to the war fighter through world-class depot maintenance, supply chain management and installation support.
AFSC – Air Force Safety Center
AFSC – Air Force Specialty Code
AFSC – Air Force Systems Command (disestablished MAJCOM; merged with AFLC in 1992 to form AFMC)
AFSFC – Air Force Security Forces Center

AFSO 21 – Air Force Smart Operations for the 21st Century
AFSOC – Air Force Special Operations Command
AFSOUTH – Air Forces Southern
AFSPC – Air Force Space Command
AFSVA – Air Force Services Agency
AFT – Alert Fire Team
AFTO – Air Force Technical Order
AFVA – Air Force Visual Aids
AFVEC – Air Force Virtual Education Center
AFWA – Air Force Weather Agency
AG (TAG) – Adjutant General, (The)
AGE – Aerospace Ground Equipment; analogous to Ground Support Equipment (GSE) in USN, USMC and USCG (Naval Aviation)
AGE Ranger – An AGE Technician
AGR – Active Guard and Reserve
AGS – Aircraft Generation Squadron
AGSM – Anti-G Straining Maneuver
AGOW – Air-Ground Operations Wing
AKRAOC – Alaska Region Air Operations Center
ALCM – Air Launched Cruise Missile
ALCON – All Concerned (used in message headers for mass emailings)
ALO – Air Liaison Officer
ALS – Airman Leadership School
AMC – Air Mobility Command
AMJAMS – Automated Military Justice Analysis and Management System
Amn – Airman; enlisted pay grade E-2
AMMO Troop – Munitions Systems Technician AMMO (U.S. Air Force)
AMMS – Airborne Missile Maintenance Squadron Missile Badge
AMS – Academy of Military Science
AMT – Aircraft Metals Technology

AMW – Air Mobility Wing
AMXS – Aircraft Maintenance Squadron
ANG – Air National Guard
ANR – Alaskan NORAD Region
AO – Authorized Outage
AOC – Air and Space Operations Center
AOG – Aircraft On Ground
AP – Air Police (Obsolete term); now called Security Forces (SF)
APS – Aerial Port Squadron
ARI – Alcohol Related Incident
ARS – (Obsolete term) Air Rescue Squadron; formerly ARRS, now known as a Rescue Squadron (RQS)
ARRS – (Obsolete term) Aerospace Rescue and Recovery Squadron
ART – AEF (Air Expeditionary Force) Reporting Tool
ART – Air Reserve Technician
ART – Armed or Alarm Response Team
ARW – Air Refueling Wing
AS – Airlift Squadron
AS – Air Station
ASAP – As Soon As Possible
ASBC – Air and Space Basic Course
ASI – Authorized Service Interruption
ASOC- Air Support Operations Center (formerly DASC- Direct Air Support Center)
ASR – Airport Surveillance Radar
ATAG – Assistant to the Adjutant General
ATC – Air traffic control
ATC – Air Training Command (disestablished MAJCOM; superseded in 1992 by AETC)
ATCALS – Air Traffic Control and Landing Systems
ATO – Air Tasking Order
ATO – Anti-Terrorism Officer
AU – Air University
AU-ABC – Air University Associate to Baccalaureate Cooperative

AW – Airlift Wing
AWACS – Airborne Warning and Control System on the E-3 Sentry aircraft
AWACS – A War Against Common Sense
AWC – Air War College
AWOL – Absent Without Leave
AWP – Awaiting Parts

B

BAH – Basic Allowance for Housing
BAS – Basic Allowance for Subsistence
BASH – Bird/Wildlife Aircraft Strike Hazard
BAQ – Bachelor Airman Quarters
BCOT – Basic Communications Officer Training
BDOC – Base Defense Operations Center
BDU – Battle Dress Uniform
BEQ – Bachelor Enlisted Quarters
BIT – Bystander Intervention Training
BITC – Base Information Transfer Center
BITS – Base Information Transfer System
BFM – Basic Fighter Maneuvers
BFT – Blue Force Tracking
BLUF – Bottom Line Up Front
BMT – Basic Military Training
BOHICA – Bend Over, Here It Comes Again; used in response to unfavorable orders.
BONE – Nickname for the B-1 Lancer, as in "B-ONE"
BOQ – Bachelor Officer Quarters
BOS – Base Operating Support
BOT – Basic Officer Training
Box Nasty – A sandwich & snack meal in a cardboard box handed out for flights
BPZ – Below Primary Zone; early promotion of an officer ahead of

peers to controlled statutory pay grades of O-4, O-5 and/or O-6
BRAC – Base Realignment and Closure
Brig Gen – Brigadier General; officer pay grade O-7
BRM – Base Records Manager
BS – Bomb Squadron
BSA – Basic Surface Attack
BTZ – Below the zone; USAF early promotion program from E-3 to E-4
BUFF – Big Ugly Fat Fucker (Nickname for Boeing B-52 Stratofortress)
BW – Bomb Wing
BX – Base Exchange (see AAFES)

C

C-Day – The unnamed day on which a deployment operation begins or is to begin
C2 – Command and Control
C4ISR – Command, Control, Communications, Computers, Intelligence, Surveillance, and Reconnaissance
CA – Combat Arms
CAF – Combat Air Force
CAFSC – Control Air Force Specialty Code
CAI – Computer Aided Instruction
CAOC – Combined Air and Space Operations Center
CAMS – Core Automated Maintenance System (database behind IMDS)
CANX - Cancelled
CAP – Civil Air Patrol, the civilian USAF Auxiliary
Capt – Captain; officer pay grade O-3
CAS – Close Air Support
CAST – Combat Airman Skills Training
CAT – Crisis Action Team
CAT – Camper Alert Team (Security Forces, Missile Field Security)

CATM – Combat Arms Training and Maintenance
CBCS – Combat Communications Squadron
CBMC – Communications Battlespace Management Course
CBT – Computer Based Training
CBRNE – Chemical, Biological, Radiological, Nuclear, and High Yield Explosives
CC – Commander
CCC - Commanders Chief
CCS - Commanders Secretary
CCAF – Community College of the Air Force
CCE – Executive Officer
CCF – First Sergeant
CCT – Combat Control
CD – Deputy Commander
CDC – Career Development Course
CE – Civil Engineering or Civil Engineers
CEG – Combat Evaluation Group
CEM – Chief Enlisted Manager
CES – Civil Engineering Squadron
CEVG – Combat Evaluation Group
CFEPT – Career Field Education and Training Plan
CFP – Communications Focal Point
CFR – Crash Fire Rescue
CFT – Cockpit Familiarization Trainer
CGO – Company Grade Officer (lieutenants and captains)
CGOC – Company Grade Officers' Council
Charlie Bravo – Cut-back, or being released early from duty
Charlie Foxtrot – Cluster Fuck
Chief – Proper term of address for Chief Master Sergeant. Also frequently used by pilots to informally refer to maintenance personnel, specifically "Crew Chiefs."
CI – Counterintelligence, Compliance Inspection
CISM – Close In Security Mobile

Class Six – BX-administered store where beer, wine & liquor is sold at a discounted price with no sales tax
CJCS – Chairman of the Joint Chiefs of Staff
CMO – Civil-Military Operations
CMO – Chief Medical Officer (term for senior medical officer at each MEPS—Military Entrance Processing Station)
CMSAF – Chief Master Sergeant of the Air Force; senior active duty enlisted member of the Air Force and a direct advisor to CSAF (holds enlisted pay grade E-9)
CMSgt – Chief Master Sergeant; enlisted pay grade E-9
CNA – Computer Network Attack
CND – Could Not Duplicate
CND – Computer Network Defense
CNO – Computer Network Operations
CNT – Counter Narco-Terror
COA – Course of Action
Col – Colonel; officer pay grade O-6
COLA – Cost of Living Adjustment
COMINT – Communications Intelligence
CONOPS – Concept of Operations
CONS – Contracting Squadron
CONUS – Continental United States
COMAFFOR – Commander, Air Force Forces
Cop – Term for Air Force Security Forces personnel
COT – Commissioned Officer Training
CPF – Civilian Personnel Flight
CPTS – Comptroller Squadron
Crew Chief – Generally used as an informal slang term for Aerospace Maintenance Personnel, AFSC 2A5. More formally used to refer to an individual in charge of an aircraft maintenance related task requiring multiple people.
CRO – Combat Rescue Officer; commissioned officer equivalent of an enlisted PJ
CRO – COMSEC Responsible Officer

CS – Communications Squadron
CSAF – Chief of Staff of the Air Force; senior ranking active duty General in USAF unless the CJCS or VCJCS post is held by a USAF General (holds officer pay grade O-10)
CSAR – Combat Search and Rescue
CSC – Central Security Control
CSS – Commander's Support Staff (orderly room)
CSO – Combat Systems Officer; a commissioned officer aeronautical rating known as Navigator until 1992
CV - Vice Commander
CUI – Combined Unit Inspection
CWO – Chief Warrant Officer; commissioned officer pay grades W-2 through W-5, currently discontinued in USAF

D

D-Day – The unnamed day on which an operation begins or is to begin
DACBT – Dissimilar Air Combat Training
DAFSC – Duty Air Force Specialty Code
DART – Dumbass Radio Troop
DAS – Date Arrived Station
DBA – Dirtbag Airman (An Airman who does not represent the Air Force Core Values)
DCO – Defensive Cyber Operations
DEAD – Destruction of Enemy Air Defenses
DEERS – Defense Eligibility Enrollment Reporting System
DEROS – Date Estimated Return from OverSeas
Dependent – Non-Military family member of a service member, typically a non-military spouse and/or children, entitled to a DD 1173 Military Dependent ID Card
DFAC – Dining Facility
DFAS – Defense Finance and Accounting Service
Dickbeaters – term referring to one's hands. Often yelled by MTIs in

the form of "pin those Dickbeaters to your side!"
DINSTAAR – Danger Is No Stranger To An AGE Ranger (See AGE)
DMSP – Defense Meteorological Satellite Program
DNIF – Duties Not Including Flying
DOE – Date of Enlistment
Dollar Ride – A pilot's first flight in an airframe
Doolie – nickname for a first year Air Force Academy cadet
DOR – Date of Rank
Double Dip – Term used for certain full-time Air Force Reserve and Air National Guard personnel when in a dual status and receiving income from two sources (e.g., Air Reserve Technician on civilian military leave as a Department of the Air Force civil servant and on concurrent active duty USAF orders)
DRSN – Defense Red Switch Network
DRU – Direct Reporting Unit
DSCS – Defense Satellite Communications System
DSD – Developmental Special Duty
DSN – Defense Switched Network
DSP – Defense Support Program
DSPD – Defense Support to Public Diplomacy
DT – Development Team
DTS – Defense Travel System
DV – Distinguished Visitor; visiting enlisted personnel in pay grade E-9, visiting officer personnel in pay grades O-6 through O-10, or visiting civilian equivalents such as GS-15, SES or politically-appointed or elected government officials
DVQ – Distinguished Visitors Quarters
DVOQ – Distinguished Visiting Officers Quarters
DWC – Deputy Wing Chaplain

E

EAD – Extended Active Duty

EADS – Eastern Air Defense Sector
ECM – Electronic Counter Measures
ECP – Entry Control Point
EELV – Evolved Expendable Launch Vehicle
EET – Exercise Evaluation Team
EFMP – Exceptional Family Member Program
EI – Engineering & Installation
EIS – Engineering & Installation Squadron
ELINT – Electronic signals Intelligence
EGI – Embedded GPS/Inertial Navigation
Embrace The Suck – Slang used among junior enlisted referencing they have little say in undesirable decisions, effectively advice that one should not worry themselves over things they cannot control
EMEDS – Expeditionary Medical Support
EMSEC – Emission Security
ENJJPT – Euro NATO Joint Jet Pilot Training
EO – Equal Opportunity
EOC – Emergency Operations Center
EOD – Explosive Ordnance Disposal
EPR – Enlisted Performance Report
ERCC – Engine Run Crew Change
E-VAR – Electronic Visitor Access Request
ERO – Engine Running Onload/Offload
EW – Electronic Warfare
EWO – Electronic Warfare Officer

F

FA – Fitness Assessment
FAA – Federal Aviation Administration
FAB – Forward Air Base
FAC – Forward Air Controller
FAIP – First Assignment Instructor Pilot
FAM – Functional Area Manager

Farts and darts – clouds and darts embroidery found on field grade and general officers' service cap visors

Fat Albert – Nickname used for the C-5A Galaxy until revoked by USAF as "derogatory". Name came from Bill Cosby's recording of "Revenge" in 1968, with the story of "Buck Buck" and Fat Albert shaking the ground as he ran.

FGO – Field Grade Officer (majors, lieutenant colonels, and colonels)

FIGMO – Fuck it I Got My Orders

Fini Flight – A pilot's last flight in the aircraft before he/she leaves a squadron, a wing, or retires from the Air Force

FLPP – Foreign Language Proficiency Pay

FM – Financial Management Comptroller

FMC – Fully Mission Capable

FMS – Foreign Military Sales

FMS – Field Maintenance Squadron

FNG – Fucking New Guy

FOA – Field Operating Agency

FOD – Foreign Object Damage or debris that can cause damage

FOUO – For Official Use Only

Four Fan Trash Can – Nickname for the C-130 Hercules

Four Fans of Freedom – Nickname for the C-130 Hercules

FRED – Fucking Ridiculous Economic Disaster (term for the C-5 Galaxy)

FS – Fighter Squadron

FSB – Force Shaping Board

FSS – Force Support Squadron

FTAC – First Term Airman's Center

FTS – Flying Training Squadron

FTU – Formal Training Unit

FTW – Flying Training Wing

FUBAR – Fucked Up Beyond All Recognition

FW – Fighter Wing

FYSA – For Your Situational Awareness

G

G-LOC – G-induced Loss of Consciousness
GBS – Global Broadcast Service (pronounced: jibz—IPA: dʒɪbz)
GC / GNC – Guidance and Control
GCCS – Global Command and Control System (pronounced: geeks—IPA: giks)
GCIC – Global Cyberspace Integration Center
GCS – Ground Control Station
GDT – Ground Data Terminal
Gen – General; officer pay grade O-10
GLCM – Ground Launched Cruise Missile
GO – General Officer; officers in pay grades O-7, O-8, O-9 and O-10 – analogous to Flag Officer in USN and USCG
GOCO – Government Owned, Contractor Operated
GOGO – Government Owned, Government Operated
GOV – Government Owned Vehicle
Gp – Group
GPC – Government Purchase Card
GPS – Global Positioning System
GTC – Government Travel Card
GuDawg- F-4 Phantom Crew Chief made of Iron (from Tae Gu ROK)
GWOT – Global War On Terrorism

H

HAF – Headquarters Air Force
HALO – High Altitude, Low Opening
HAHO – High Altitude, High Opening
Hangar "[#]" – A nonexistent hangar (e.g., if there are 4 hangars, then it would be Hangar 5); heard most often over radios as slang code for latrine/bathroom/Porta John. Example: "Get me to Hangar 5!"
HARM – High Speed Anti-Radiation Missile

HARM – Host Aviation Resource Management
HARRT – Humanitarian Assistance Rapid Response Team
Hawg – Nickname for the A-10 Thunderbolt II
HAZCON – Hazardous Condition
HC – Chaplain Headquarters
HIA – Held in Abeyance
HO – Historian's Office
HPC – Historic Properties Custodian
HTS – HARM Targeting System
HUA – Heard, Understood, Acknowledged
HUAW – Hurry Up and Wait
HUD – Head-Up Display
HUMINT – Human Intelligence

I

IA – Information Assurance
IAW – In Accordance With
ICBM – Intercontinental Ballistic Missile
ID 10 T Problem – A problem that is created by an "idiot"
IFE – In-Flight Emergency
IFF – Identification Friend or Foe
IFF – Introduction to Fighter Fundamentals
IFFCC – Integrated Flight and Fire Control Computer
IFS – Introductory Flight Screening
IFT – Introductory Flight Training
IG – Inspector General
ILS – Instrument landing system
IMDS – Integrated Maintenance Database System
IMINT – Imagery Intelligence
INOP – Inoperative/Inoperable
INOSC – Integrated Network Operations and Security Center
IP – Instructor Pilot
IPB – Intelligence Preparation of the Battlespace

IO – Information Operations
IOC – Initial Operational Capability
IOIC – Information Operations Integration Course
IS – Intelligence Squadron
ISR – Intelligence, Surveillance, and Reconnaissance
ITT – Information, Tickets, and Travel
IYAAYAS – If You Ain't Ammo, You Ain't Shit
IYAAYWOT – If You Ain't Ammo, You're Waitin' On Them

J

J-STARS – Joint Surveillance Target Attack Radar System on the E-8 JSTARS aircraft
JA – Judge Advocate
JA/ATT – Joint Airborne/ Air Transportability Training
JAOC – Joint Air and Space Operations Center
JATO – Jet-Assisted Take-Off
JDAM – Joint Direct Attack Munition
JEEP – Just Enough Education To Pass
JEEP – Just Entering Electronic Principals
JEEP – Just Educated Enough to Post (Security Forces)
JFACC – Joint Forces Air Component Commander
JEIM – Jet Engine Intermediate Maintenance
JOAP – Joint Oil Analysis Program
JOPES – Joint Operation Planning and Execution System
JPATS – Joint Primary Air Training System
JPME – Joint Professional Military Education
JPPT – Joint Primary Pilot Training
JSF – Joint Strike Fighter
JSOW – Joint Standoff Weapon
JSUPT – Joint Specialized Undergraduate Pilot Training
JWICS – Joint Worldwide Intelligence Communications System

K

KISS – Keep It Simple Stupid

L

LAPES – Low Altitude Parachute Extraction System.
LATN – Low Altitude Tactical Navigation.
Lawn Dart – Nickname for F-16 Fighting Falcon or any other fast, pointy-nosed, single-engine fighter aircraft.
LCAP – Logistics Compliance Assessment Program.
LEAP – Language Enabled Airman Program.
LFE - Large Formation Exercise
LG – Logistics Group.
LGB – Laser-Guided Bomb.
LIFT – Lead In Fighter Training.
LIMFAC – Limiting Factor.
Linda Lovelace (Reference to the C-5 Galaxy aircraft, because it kneels and takes it from both ends.)
LMR – Land Mobile Radio
LOA – Letter of Admonishment.
LOA – Letter of Appreciation.
LOAC – Law of Armed Conflict.
LOC – Letter of Counseling.
LOGI – Logistics NCOIC (Squadron, Group, Wing).
LOR – Letter of Reprimand.
LOWAT – Low Altitude Training.
LRS – Logistics Readiness Squadron.
LT – Familiar term for a Lieutenant, Second or First; usually used as a form of address by those under his/her command.
Lt Col – Lieutenant Colonel; officer pay grade O-5.
Lt Gen – Lieutenant General; officer pay grade O-9.
LWOP – Leave Without Pay.

M

MAC – Military Airlift Command (disestablished MAJCOM)
MAF – Mobility Air Force
Maj – Major; officer pay grade O-4
Maj Gen – Major General; officer pay grade O-8
MAJCOM – Major Command
MANPADS – Man-Portable Air Defense System
MARE – Major Accident Response Exercise
MASINT – Measurement and Signature Intelligence
MATS – Military Air Transport Service (disestablished command, superseded by MAC and then AMC
MDG – Medical Group
MDS – Mission Design Series of aircraft; analogous to T/M/S for Type/Model/Series in USN & USMC (Naval Aviation)
MEO – Military Equal Opportunity
MEPS – Military Entrance Processing Station
METL – Mission Essential Task Listing
MFLC – Military and Family Life Counselor
MFH – Military Family Housing
MFT – Mobile Fire Team
MICAP – Mission Incapable
MICT – Management Internal Control Toolset
MIF – Maneuver Item File
MILDEC – Military Deception
MILSTRIP – Military Standard Requisitioning and Issue Procedure
MLR – Management Level Review
MOAB – Massive Ordnance Air Blast Bomb/Mother Of All Bombs
MOOTW – Military Operations Other than War
MOS – Maintenance Operations Squadron
Mosquito Wings – Nickname for the Airman rank insignia
MPF – Military Personnel Flight
MRE – Meal Ready to Eat
MS – Missile Squadron
MSG – Mission Support Group
MSME – Medical Standard Management Element

MSgt – Master Sergeant; enlisted pay grade E-7
MSS – Mission Support Squadron
MTI – Military Training Instructor
MTL – Military Training Leader
Mud Hen – Nickname for the F-15E Strike Eagle
MW – Missile Wing
MWR – Morale, Welfare and Recreation
MWS – Major Weapons System
MX – Maintenance
MXG – Maintenance Group
MXS – Maintenance Squadron

N

NAF – Numbered Air Force
Nav – Navigator, now known since 2009 as a Combat Systems Officer
NCC – Network Control Center
NCO – Non-commissioned Officer
NCOA – Non-commissioned Officer Academy
NCOIC – Non-Commissioned Officer in Charge
NCW – Network-Centric Warfare
NDI – Nondestructive Inspection
NEADS – Northeast Air Defense Sector
NGB – National Guard Bureau
NIPR – Non-secure Internet Protocol (IP) Router Network
NKAWTG – Nobody Kicks Ass Without Tanker Gas
NMC – Non Mission Capable
NMSA – Non-Nuclear Munitions Storage Area
NMUSAF – National Museum of the United States Air Force
Nonner – "Non-sortie generating." Derogatory term used by aircraft maintenance personnel when referring to enlisted and officers who are not directly involved in aircraft maintenance or manning aircraft

Non-rated Officer – USAF commissioned officer not holding an aeronautical rating
NOSC – Network Operations and Security Center
NOTAM – Notice To Airmen
NSI – Nuclear Surety Inspection
NVG – Night Vision Goggles
NUB – New Useless Bitch (reference for new person on station; contraction from newbie (which was originally new boy), and then backronymed)

O

OA – Occupational Analysis
OA – Outstanding Airman
OAPT – Officer Awaiting Pilot Training.
OAPTer – An officer in OAPT status. While other 2nd Lt's begin their flight training, non-flying technical training and/or initial leadership roles, OAPTers complete menial tasks in support of the mission while they wait for their assigned training date (this is known as "casual status"). It is important for all operational bases, as OAPTers are most often supplemental to the assigned commissioned officer workforce.
OAR – Occupational Analysis Report
OAY – Outstanding Airman of the Year
OAYA – Outstanding Airman of the Year Award
OCO – Offensive Cyber Operations
OCONUS – Outside the Continental United States
OCR – Office of Collateral Responsibility
OFO – Out Fucking Off
OG – Operations Group
OIC – Officer in Command
OL – Operating Location
OODA – Observe Orient Decide Act
OPCON – Operational Control

OPR – Office of Primary Responsibility
OPR – Officer Performance Report
OPSEC – Operations Security
OPTN – Operationalizing and Professionalizing the Network
ORI – Operational Readiness Inspection
ORM – Operation Risk Management
OSI – Office of Special Investigation
OSR – Occupational Survey Report
OSS – Operations Support Squadron
OT&E – Operational Test and Evaluation
OTS – Officer Training School

P

PA – Public Affairs
PACAF – Pacific Air Forces
PAFSC – Primary Air Force Specialty Code
PAR – Precision Approach Radar
PAS – Political Affairs Strategist
PAX – Air passengers
PCS – Permanent Change of Station
PDS – Permanent Duty Station
PERSCO – Personnel Support for Contingency Operations
Perpes – Humorous nickname for PRP, takeoff on herpes
PFE – Promotion Fitness Examination
PFM – Pure Fucking Magic; Term to refer to a technical problem that somehow resolved itself
PFT – Physical Fitness Test
PICNIC – Problem In Chair, Not In Computer; Used by help desk personnel to indicate user ignorance
PING – Person In Need of Graduation
PITT – Person In need of Technical Training
PJ – Pararescueman
PMC – Partially Mission Capable

PME – Professional Military Education
PMEL – Precision Measurement Equipment Laboratory
Pocket Rocket – Term for the missile badge on the uniforms of current and former ICBM and cruise missile launch operations and missile maintenance personnel
POL – Petroleum, Oils, & Lubricants, the traditional name for the Fuels Management Flight
Pop Tart – Airman whose technical career schools are 6 weeks or less
posn – position
Prime Beef – Prime Base Engineer Emergency Force
PRF – Promotion Recommendation Form
PRP – Personnel Reliability Program
PSDM – Personnel Services Delivery Memorandum
PSYOP – Psychological Operations
PTL – Physical Training Leader

Q

QAF – Quality Air Force
Queep – A task or duty that is completely useless and ultimately unrelated to your primary job. It is often assigned by superiors not of your career field as they assume that you have time to constantly work these tasks. Example: "I have a lot of queep to do before I go home." "I need to finish all of this queep before I can go fly."

R

RA – Resource Advisor
RAF – Royal Air Force
Rainbow Flight – Fresh trainees at BMT who have not yet received uniforms (clothing colors represent the rainbow)
RAM – Random Antiterrorism Measure
RAPCON – Radar Approach Control
RAS – Regional Affairs Strategist

Rated Officer – USAF commissioned officer holding an aeronautical rating as a Pilot (to include Astronaut), Combat Systems Officer (to include Astronaut), Navigator (to include Astronaut), Air Battle Manager, Observer (Astronaut) or Flight Surgeon
RED HORSE – Rapid Engineer Deployable Heavy Operational Repair Squadron Engineers
RET, Ret, (Ret) – Designations for retired military personnel, typically following the service designation in a title, e.g., Col USAF (Ret)
RF – Radio frequency
RFF – Request [F]or Forces (initiated by Army)
RHIP – "Rank Has Its Privileges"
RIF – Reduction In Force
RIP – Report on Individual Personnel
RNLTD – Report No Later Than Date
ROAD – Retired On Active Duty
RON – Remain overnight
ROTC – Reserve Officers' Training Corps
RPA – Remotely Piloted Aircraft
RQG – Rescue Group
RQS – Rescue Squadron (formerly ARS)
RQW – Rescue Wing
RTB – Return To Base
RTIC – Real Time In the Cockpit
RS – Reconnaissance Squadron
RW – Reconnaissance Wing

S

SAASS – School of Advanced Air and Space Studies
SABC – Self Aid Buddy Care
SAC – Strategic Air Command (disestablished MAJCOM)
SAF/SECAF – Secretary of the Air Force
SAM – Surface to Air Missile
SAPR – Sexual Assault Prevention and Response

SARC – Sexual Assault Response Coordinator
SATCOM – Satellite Communications
SAV – Staff Assistance Visit
SBIRS – Space-Based Infrared System
SCOD – Static Close Out Date
SDF – Standard Deployment Folder
SEAD – Suppression of Enemy Air Defenses (pronounced "seed")
SEADS – Southeast Air Defense Sector
SEI – Special Experience Identifier
Secret Squirrel stuff – Material classified above secret or special compartmentalized information.
Senior – Informal shortening for Senior Master Sergeant
SEPCOR – Separate Correspondence
SERE – Survival, Evasion, Resistance and Escape
SF – Security Forces
SFS – Security Forces Squadron
Sgt – Sergeant; a since discontinued additional rank in enlisted pay grade E-4 from 1976 to 1991
Shirt – A unit first sergeant
Short – Close to a PCS date or retirement
Sierra Hotel (SH) – Shit Hot
SIGINT – Signals Intelligence
SIPR – Secret Internet Protocol
SKT – Specialty Knowledge Test
Slick Sleeve – Nickname for an Airman Basic (owing to the absence of rank insignia on an individual's sleeve)
SLUF – Short Little Ugly Fucker (Derogatory nickname for the LTV A-7 Corsair II)
SME – Subject Matter Expert
SMSgt – Senior Master Sergeant, enlisted pay grade E-8
SNAFU – Situation Normal All Fucked Up
SNCO – Senior Non-commissioned Officer; enlisted pay grades E-7, E-8 and E-9
SNCOA – Senior Non-commissioned Officer Academy

Snacko – A highly underestimated, mission critical position held most often by newly reported Lieutenants in a flying squadron. Doing well at the Snacko position will prompt one for a laudable career. Failing at such a job will often entail severe ridicule and, if necessary, replacement and retraining by the flying squadron.

Snuffy – Generic term given to any Airmen of lower rank. "And here came Airman Snuffy late to the party as usual."

SOP – Standard Operating Procedure

SOPS – Space Operations Squadron

SOS – Squadron Officer School

SOS – Special Operations Squadron

SOW – Special Operations Wing

SOWT - Special Operations Weather Technician

Spark Chaser – Nickname for aircraft maintenance personnel dealing with electronic, non-mechanical systems

Spirit Mission – A good-natured act, commonly in the form of a prank, banner, or...reacquisition...of a person/thing, to show pride for a group of individuals. Usually harmless.

Sq – Squadron

SrA – Senior Airman; enlisted pay grade E-4

SRC – Solid Rock Cafe (new as of 2011, located at Sheppard Air Force Base, TX – unofficial anogram that is used by officers as well as students)

SRT – Security Response Team

SSgt – Staff Sergeant; enlisted pay grade E-5

SST – Supervisor Safety Training

Staff – Informal shortening for Staff Sergeant

STEP – Stripe Through Exceptional Performance

Stick Actuator – Pilot

Stink Bug – Nickname for the F-117 Nighthawk

Strike Eagle – Nickname for the F-15E Strike Eagle

STS – Special Tactics Squadron

sUAS - Small Unmanned Aircraft System

SURF – Single Uniform Request Format

SVS – Services Squadron
SW – Space Wing
SWA – Southwest Asia
SWAG – Scientific Wild-Ass Guess
SWO – Staff Weather Officer

T

T&A – Test and Acceptance
TAC – Tactical Air Command (disestablished MAJCOM)
TAC-P – Tactical Air Control Party
TACAN – Tactical Air Navigation
TACON – Tactical Control
TAFCSD – Total Active Federal Commission Service Date
TAFMSD – Total Active Federal Military Service Date
TAG (AG) – The Adjutant General
Tail-End Charlie – Person bringing up the rear of a formation or a tail gunner
TAP – Transition Assistance Program
TBA – Training Business Area
TCNO – Time Compliance Network Order
TCTO – Time Compliance Technical Order
TDY – Temporary Duty; analogous to Temporary Additional Duty (TAD / TEMADD) in USN, USMC and USCG
Tech – Informal shortening of Technical Sergeant
TFCSD – Total Federal Commissioned Service to Date
TGP – Targeting Pod
TIG – The Inspector General
TLAR – That Looks About Right
TLF – Temporary Living Facility
TO – Technical Order
TOT – Time Over Target
Tracking – Reference to offensive avionics on combat aircraft.

Following and understanding the subject at hand. (IE: "I need this done yesterday, Airman. Are you tracking?")
TRF – Tactical Response Force
TRG – Training Group
TRS – Training Squadron
TRW – Training Wing
TSgt – Technical Sergeant; enlisted pay grade E-6
TST – Time-Sensitive Target
TTP – Tactics, Techniques, and Procedures
TU – Tango Uniform, slang for 'tits up'.

U

UAS – unmanned aircraft system
UAV – unmanned aerial vehicle
UCI – unit compliance inspection
UCSOT – Undergraduate Combat Systems Officer Training
UHT – Undergraduate Helicopter Pilot Training
UIF – unfavorable information file
ULN – unit line number
UMD – unit manpower document
UNT – Undergraduate Navigator Training (superseded by UCSOT)
UNWT – Undergraduate Network Warfare Training
UPT – Undergraduate Pilot Training (superseded by ENJJPT, JSUPT and UHT)
USAF – United States Air Force
USAFA – United States Air Force Academy
USAFE – United States Air Forces in Europe
USAFEC – United States Air Force Expeditionary Center
USAFR – United States Air Force Reserve
USAFWC – United States Air Force Warfare Center

V

VAQ – visiting airman quarters
VFR – visual flight rules
Viper – nickname for the F-16 Fighting Falcon
VML – vulnerable to move list
vMPF – virtual military personnel flight
VOQ – visiting officer quarters
VOR – VHF omnidirectional range
V/R – virtual regards / very respectfully (closing salutation)
vRED – virtual record of emergency data
VSP – voluntary separation pay

W

WADS – Western Air Defense Sector
WAF – Women in the Air Force
WAG – wild-ass guess
WAPS – Weighted Airman Promotion System
WASP – Women Airforce Service Pilots
WC – wing chaplain
WG – wing
WIC – weapons instructor course
WIT – wing inspection team
Winchester – out of ammo
WOWWAJAA – with out weapons we are just another airline
WRM – war reserve material
WRT – with regard to / with reference to
WSA – weapons storage area
WSO – weapon systems officer
WX – weather

X

X-plane – experimental aircraft
XP3 - disposable item

Y

Y-plane – prototype aircraft

Z

Zero – officer
Zoo – nickname for the Air Force Academy
Zoomie – nickname for an Air Force Academy graduate or cadet

ACKNOWLEDGMENTS

I wish to thank a few people who helped my flying career, whether they realise it or not, our fun conversations or the serious chats we had and the discussions around flying, made this book possible.

As I worked through the list of everyone who has influenced my aviation career, it is incredible to see the number of people I will always be grateful to. Thank you.

Neville Swan (first gliding instructor)
Craig McNeal (first power flying instructor)
Aaron Shipman
Aaron 'AJ' Jeffery
Aaron Pearce
Aaron Marshall
Adam Eltham
Aiden Campbell
Alan Beck QSM
Alistair Blake
Amiria Wallis

Anastasios Raptis
Andrew Gormlie
Andrew Hope
Andrew Lorimer
Andrew Love
Andrew Sunde
Andrew Telfer
Andy Mackay
Andy Stevenson MNZM
Angelo Cruz
Ben Lee
Ben Marcus
Ben Pryor NZGM
Benjamin James
Bevan Dewes
Bill Reid
Bradley Marsh
Brett Emeny
Brett Nicholls
Bruce Lynch
Bryn Lockie
Carlo Santoro
Chantel Strooh
Charles J Cook
Chris Barry
Chris Bromley
Chris Pond
Chris Satler
Chris Sperou OAM
Christina Harvey
Christoph Berthoud
Conor Neill
Cosmo Mead
Craig Piner

Craig Rook
Craig Speck
Craig Steel
Craig Walecki
Damien Campbell
Daniel Campbell
Darren Crabb
Daryl Gillett
Dave Blackwell
David Brown
Dave Campbell
Dave Cogan
Dave Hayman
Dave Rouse
David Lowy AM
David Morgan
David Saunders
David Wilkinson
Dennis Eckhoff
Derry Belcher
Desmond Barry
Don Lockie
Donovan Burns
Doug Batten
Doug Brown
Doug Burrell
Dwight Weston
Enya Mae McPherson
Eric Morgan
Eva Keim
Flo Smith
Frank Parker
Gareth Wheeler
Gavin Conroy

Gavin Trethewey
Gavin Weir
Gene De Marco
Geoff Cooper
George Oldfield JP
Giovanni Nustrini
Graeme 'Spud' Spurdle
Graham Lake
Graham Nevill
Graham Orphan
Grant Armishaw
Grant 'Muddy' Murdoch
Greg Quinn
Guy Bourke
Harvey Lockie
Hayden Leech
HH Prince Faisal bin Abdulla bin Mohammed Saud
Ian Lilley
Ian 'Iggy' Wood
Imogen Ling
James Aldridge
Jamie Wagner
Jason Alexander
Jason Haggitt DSD
Jay McIntyre
Jed Melling
Jill McCaw
Jim Rankin DSD
Jock MacLachlan
Joe Oldfield
John Duxfield ARCOM
John Gemmell
John Lamont
John Martin

John McCaw
Jonathan Bowen
Joseph D'Ath
Josh Camp
Juan Ferandoes
Jurgis Kairys
Karl Stol
Keith McKenzie QSM
Keith Skilling
Keith Stephens
Kenny Love
Kermit Weeks
Kevin Langley
Kevin Vile
Kirsty Coleman
Kishan Bhashyam
Kris Vette
Lawrence Acket
Liberio Riosa
Lionel Page
Liz King (Mother Goose)
Lloyd Galloway
Loïc Ifrah
Louisa 'Choppy' Patterson
Malcolm Clement
Martin Schulze
Mark Helliwell
Mark Lowndes
Mary Patterson
Matt Hall
Matt Ledger
Maurizio Folini
Melissa Andrzejewski (nee Pemberton)
Michael Bach

Michael Jeffs
Mike Clark
Mike Foster
Mike Harvey
Mike Jorgenson
Mike Read
Mike Slack
Nando Parrado
Nathan Graves
Nick Cree
Nick Tarascio
Nigel Cooper
Nigel Lamb
Nina Hayman
Paul Andronicou
Paul 'Huggy' Hughan
Paul 'Simmo' Simmons AM CSM
Pete Meadows
Pete Pring Shambler
Peter Harper
Peter Jefferies
Peter Thorpe
Phil Freeman
Phill Hooker
Pip Borrman
Ray Burns
Ray Richards
Reuben Muir
Rex Pemberton
Richard Button
Richard Hectors
Richard Hood
Rev. Dr Richard Waugh QSM
Richie McCaw ONZ

Rick Watson
Rob Fox
Rob Fry
Rob Mackley
Rob Neil
Rob Owens
Rob Weavers
Robert Burns
Roy Crane
Roy Cunningham
Ruan Heynike
Ruth Nisbet
Ryan Brooks
Ryan Francis
Sam Elimelech
Scott 'Macka' McKenzie
Sean Perrett
Shaun Clark
Shaun Roseveare
Simon J Gault
Simon Lockie
Simon Mundell
Simone Moro
SQNLDR Les Munro CNZM DSO QSO DFC JP
Steve Ahrens
Steve Wallace
Stephen Boyce
Stephen Death
Steve Gibson
Steve Newland
Steve Jurd
Steven Perreau
Stu Wards
Tasos Raptis

Tee Jay Sullivan
Tim Marshall
Sir Tim Wallis
Todd O'Hara
Tracy Dixon
Wayne Fowler
Wayne Ormrod
Wayne Thompson
Vaughan Davis
Yoshihide 'Yoshi' Muroya

ABOUT THE AUTHOR

With a passion for aviation passed on from his father who worked in the National Airways Corporation in New Zealand, Fletcher grew up with the aim of becoming a pilot in the RNZAF.

Fletcher first flew solo in a glider at the age of 16, and after winning the RNZAF Flying Scholarship, he flew solo in the Air Tourer. He tried parachuting several dozen times, before graduating onto paragliding, and finally obtained his Private Pilots License.

He is the producer of the global television show *FlightPathTV*, on air in over sixty countries, and travels extensively interviewing pilots from around the world.

With twenty years experience working with global entrepreneurs through EO (Entrepreneurs Organisation), Fletcher trains entrepreneurs to experience share between each other, to learn from any mistakes. From here, the idea of the *Lessons From The Sky* series was born.

Fletcher has selected and compiled these stories to help pilots learn from others — to ensure the safety of current and future pilots in the skies.

www.fletchermckenzie.com

www.ingramcontent.com/pod-product-compliance
Lightning Source LLC
Chambersburg PA
CBHW020417010526
44118CB00010B/294